The
GOLDEN AGE
of CRICKET

The
GOLDEN AGE
of CRICKET

George Plumptre

Macdonald
Queen Anne Press

A QUEEN ANNE PRESS BOOK

© George Plumptre 1990

First published in Great Britain in 1990 by
Queen Anne Press, a division of
Macdonald & Co (Publishers) Ltd
Orbit House
1 New Fetter Lane
London EC4A 1AR

A member of Maxwell Macmillan Pergamon Publishing Corporation

Jacket design – Judith Clarke
Book design – Judith Clarke and Michael Harris

British Library Cataloguing in Publication Data
Plumptre, George
   The golden age of cricket.
   1. Cricket, history
   I. Title
   796.35809

ISBN 0-356-17939-7

Typeset by MS Filmsetting Limited, Frome
Printed and bound in Great Britain by Butler and Tanner Ltd, Frome

Picture credits

Author's Collection: 23, 43, 75.

George Beldam Collection: 113.

Eton College Collection: 169.

Hulton-Deutsch Collection: 11, 12, 19, 21, 35, 57, 79, 89, 93, 94, 100, 104, 115, 121, 124, 142, 179, 182.

Kent CCC: front cover, 147.

Roger Mann Collection: 9, 13, 16, 26, 27, 30, 37, 42, 46 left, 48, 55, 60, 63, 64, 65, 70, 72, 73, 84, 85, 97, 98, 101, 108, 119, 129, 131, 136, 142, 143, 144, 154, 157, 159, 161, 163, 165, 166, 170, 177, 183.

Courtesy of the MCC: 10, 15, 17, 25, 33, 41, 46, 49, 52, 53, 59, 61, 67, 68, 77, 82, 88, 91, 96, 103, 106, 110, 112, 113, 117, 118, 123, 126, 128, 132, 135, 137, 138, 140–1, 145, 149, 151, 156, 160, 164, 168, 172, 173, 175.

Private Collection: 44, 45.

Courtesy of J.W.H. O'Regan: 69.

Surrey CCC: 54.

CONTENTS

ACKNOWLEDGEMENTS

My main debt of thanks is to Jim Swanton for allowing me unlimited access to his library of cricket books – in particular his set of *Wisden* – and for giving me the benefit of many hours of discussion and his reminiscences. Peter Wynne-Thomas provided me with invaluable information about amateurs and professionals as well as a quantity of facts and anecdotes to do with Nottinghamshire. I would also like to thank the following people for their help: Leslie Ames, John Bright-Holmes, Aidan Crawley, Neville Ford, Joe Hardstaff, Lord Home of the Hirsel, E.H. Spooner and R.E.S. Wyatt. For the illustrations I am particularly indebted to Kent CCC for the photograph reproduced on the front of the jacket, to Stephen Green and the MCC, Roger Mann, and Anne-Marie Ehrlich for her picture research. Finally my thanks to Lorraine Jerram at Queen Anne Press and to my agent, Vivienne Schuster.

George Plumptre
Rowling, Kent

JANUARY 1990

INTRODUCTION
A CULT OF NOSTALGIA

It would not be an exaggeration to say that the cataclysm of the First World War and the writing of Neville Cardus combined to shroud the cricket of the Edwardian era in a cult of nostalgia. The First World War brought to an abrupt end a way of life which, in retrospect, could not have gone on anyway, but the manner in which it was extinguished left it with an aura of glamour which a natural, slower death might have tarnished. During the four years of war, cricketers were not spared any more than anybody else and when peace returned and the game was revived in 1919 most people looked back to what had been lost rather than forward to future prospects.

Meanwhile the pen of Neville Cardus was beginning to work and while his column in the *Manchester Guardian*, written under the pseudonym 'Cricketer', was primarily concerned with the cricket of the day, it was not long before he found time to express his feelings about the period when, as a boy, he had watched cricket at Old Trafford. *Days In the Sun*, containing a number of essays about the Edwardian heroes and matches, was published in 1924 and *Cricket*, published in 1930, is filled with glowing references – comparing the past in an unquestionably favourable light to the present – of which a few extracts give the flavour.

Discussing Jessop's innings at The Oval in 1902 he wrote, 'This innings by Jessop had immortal longings; it will never be forgotten. The vision, the undying chivalry of it, belong not only to cricket, but to the unwritten saga of the English people; less worthy themes have served the bardic strain.' He wondered whether he dreamt of or actually saw Reggie Spooner 'the Herrick of cricket' and Archie MacLaren 'magnificent in his ambition and reckless in his sovereignty', and of the period as a whole he had 'the evidence of "Wisden", to reassure me that in every limb of cricket there ran warm, original blood'.

Cardus was by no means the only cricket writer or historian between the wars discussing the Edwardian age. In H.S. Altham's standard work, *A History of Cricket*, published in 1926, there were equally laudatory descriptions of the period. But no one had ever written about cricket quite like this before, and it was Cardus's language as much as his content which established his reputation and, at the same time, was decisive in guaranteeing the great Edwardian cricketers some sort of immortality. They, their matches and the standards of their time, became the yardstick by which others should be judged and, by common consent, usually failed to match up.

One thing is quite certain, the Edwardians themselves would not have thanked Cardus for tinting posterity's view of them. Confident, self-assured and robust they would have considered that their achievements were more than capable of speaking for themselves, even over an ever-increasing distance of time. They had no illusions about their talent or relative lack of it and there was nothing remotely self-conscious about the manner in which they played their cricket. MacLaren strode to the wicket and batted like a feudal knight, not because of some glorified image of batsmanship, but because it suited his pugnacious nature to do so and because it was how he considered bowlers should be treated. The great Surrey fast bowler Tom Richardson did not bound in to bowl often more than a thousand overs in a season because he considered his role to be that of a cricketing workhorse. He did so because his enormous strength and appetite for his craft enabled him to continue to threaten batsmen long after most men would have limped off the field exhausted.

Continuing with the same examples, Cardus was often at his most lyrical when writing about his adored trilogy of Lancashire's first three batsmen, Spooner, MacLaren and Tyldesley, but the most striking feature of the trio was their originality. Three of the acknowledged best of their time, each batted in his own contrasting manner and the differences were instantly discernible. None ever felt either the need or the inclination to emulate the others. Similarly, Richardson never had as lethal a slow ball as his Surrey partner of some seasons, Bill Lockwood, but he never felt the urge to copy the latter's secret weapon.

It is because of their vigour and originality that the cricketers of the Edwardian era remain refreshing some 75 years after the end of their period, and these qualities do not require a nostalgic view to be appreciated. Their exploits and matches are part of history but the lessons that they taught and the revolutionary progress that was made during their two decades remain very real today. They were fortunate enough to be playing during the period when modern cricket was being formulated in supremely receptive surroundings. At a time when there are staleness and a lack of confidence or sense of direction in cricket, they and their era are an enjoyable and stimulating subject.

1

THE EDWARDIAN ETHOS

Cricket as an integral part of the national way of life achieved a pinnacle during the Edwardian era. The foundations of the game itself had been laid during the preceding decades of the nineteenth century, but it was the manner in which cricket struck a chord at all levels of society, and responded to economic developments conducive to its expansion, which were decisive. Organized sport in general assumed a vital position in the ethos of the age and cricket enjoyed unrivalled popularity as the summer game, both for players and spectators.

Bolstered by years of Victorian prosperity and stability, and deriving a sense of superiority from England's imperial and naval power, Edwardians were confident, vigorous and competitive. Sporting prowess was universally admired and pursued with enormous zest. They had both the motivation and the time to indulge in perfecting the techniques of a chosen sport and in so doing to raise it to a level of performance that would inevitably appeal to ever-increasing and appreciative audiences.

Ranji and friends ready for weekend parties and some cricket.

The Golden Age of Cricket

Ranji, the Indian prince who played for England and the cricketing acme of
imperial Edwardianism.

Cricket was to enjoy a place of unique importance for many reasons, not least because it was so compatible with and closely attuned to the mood of the period. Its leisured pace and stylized method were both characteristics which were, on a larger scale, at the heart of the Edwardian way of life. The opportunities it presented for the contrast of elegant and effortless batsmanship set against aggressive fast bowling appealed instinctively, for physical talent and strength were prized qualities. Many a lady sighed with anticipation at the sight of Tom Richardson or Sammy Woods bowling, only a few seconds later to clap with delight as the ball was stroked through the covers by the slight figure of Reggie Spooner or Ranjitsinhji.

The Edwardians loved dressing up, to which end cricket was ideally suited. White flannels were immaculately pressed and many amateurs followed Ranjitsinhji's example of wearing a silk shirt. Adornment was provided by brightly coloured silk neckbands worn round the waist instead of a belt, caps and blazers. Never before or since have such displays of different club colours been put on show, so that, for instance, it was quite likely at a Gentlemen v. Players match for the Gentlemen to take the field each in a different coloured cap.

The professionals were more modest in their attire but, especially off the field, often followed the amateurs' sartorial example. Wilfred Rhodes's biographer Sidney Rogerson recalled travelling by train with the Yorkshireman in 1907.

> He was wearing a well-cut grey flannel suit. His brown shoes shone with much polishing and his straw hat had the scarlet and yellow band of MCC, or else he was wearing an MCC tie, I forget which. With his deeply tanned face he looked, I remember thinking, almost exactly like the young captain in the 60th Rifles who used when on leave from India to attend the parish church.

The immaculate professional, Wilfred Rhodes, as described by his biographer, Sidney Rogerson.

The Australian Albert Trott, who played for Middlesex,
was less interested in appearances.

Not everyone put such store by their appearance however, as Cyril Foley recalled about the Australian Albert Trott's first game for Middlesex at the beginning of the 1898 season. It was a bitterly cold day at Lord's and Foley remembered that one of the Middlesex amateurs, Timothy O'Brien, was fielding in an ulster, but Trott 'was clad in a flannel shirt that had been washed so often that you could see his skin through it and wore no sweater. An ominous black cloud appeared over the practice ground. I drew Trott's attention to it and said: "It's going to snow." ' Presumably Foley was hoping that the Australian would show some concern and even possibly resort to wearing a sweater. Not a bit of it. 'Trott gazed at the cloud. "I hope it is" he said, "I've never seen snow." '

Appearances were equally important for spectators. Some matches, in particuiar the leading fixtures at Lord's – Gentlemen v. Players, Oxford v. Cambridge and Eton v. Harrow – became major events in Edwardian society's annual calendar, a part of 'the Season' rivalled only by Royal Ascot. For men morning dress with top hats was *de rigueur*, while the ladies vied with each other in their display of enormous hats and rustling full-length frocks. Later in the summer the atmosphere was more relaxed but equally elegant at the festivals such as Scarborough or the week at Canterbury where the atmosphere was comparable to the late summer race-meeting at Goodwood. Such ritualization, the elevation of a sporting event into a social occasion, was something at which the Edwardians were unsurpassed.

Life in Edwardian England was formalized by class distinctions. However different from conditions of life today, it would be misleading to judge the period by contemporary standards, for while the barriers were very real they were by and large accepted as inevitable. One of cricket's major successes was that within the well-ordered framework of social life it reached across the barriers and in so doing achieved genuine and deep-rooted popularity. As Eric Midwinter wrote in his biography of W.G. Grace, 'Cricket was so appropriate to the age because, crucially, professional and amateur played *together* and jointly entertained both classes from which they sprang.' He illustrates the point by quoting W.S. Gilbert's adage that it 'provided rump steak for the gallery and oyster sauce for the stalls'.

The distinction between amateurs and professionals dominated English cricket during the Edwardian age, but in a manner that was productive rather than divisive. Obviously there were grievances, and the details of distinction are often dismissed today as petty, pedantic and – as far as the professionals were concerned – demeaning. Certainly many members of visiting Australian sides, all of whom played as amateurs, felt that they were. But it was inevitable that the regulations that delineated life in general would apply both on and off the cricket field.

Stilted and unnatural though the superficial formalities may have been, they enabled a social fusion to occur which distinguished cricket from any other sport and which accounted for both the kaleidoscope of talent at the game's highest levels and its extraordinary breadth of establishment. A public-school match at Lord's or a country-house match in Kent were a world apart from the unromantic competitiveness of a Saturday afternoon colliery match at Sutton-in-Ashfield, or a Lancashire league game in Burnley or Bacup. But from these hugely diverse backgrounds came the men who together played first-class cricket, who forged some of the strongest England sides ever known, and who brought to the game their own particular individuality.

A Kent group in 1897: amateurs in boaters and blazers – mostly the grey and black stripes of the Band of Brothers – professionals in caps and shirtsleeves.

The Victorians attempted to instil into the game of cricket a moral significance which at times erred towards cant, as was described some years later by Neville Cardus:

> The Victorians so endowed the game with their own moral grandeur that to this day the president of Little Puddleton cricket club cannot take the chair at the annual meeting without telling his audience that cricket is 'synonymous' with straight conduct, honour bright, and all the other recognized Christian virtues . . .

Cardus goes on to pose the question, 'Why should a cricketer be especially singled out because he plays by the rules? And why, when footballers and jockeys "play the game", why are they not applauded likewise, and their games exalted to the realms of the ethical?'

There is no doubt, however, that cricket did possess a special significance compared to other sports, although how much this was intrinsic to its make-up or read into it by the Victorians is debatable. The significance stemmed from the fact that the game promoted a code of conduct, a type of behaviour and the pursuit of certain goals which were ideally compatible with the Victorian outlook on life. Its promotion as a pastime that was physically and mentally beneficial — to both upper- and middle-class boys as part of their formal education at school and university, and working-class boys and young men aspiring to escape from the squalor and hardship of their normal lives — was commendable, so long as realism prevailed. This meant teaching Grantland Rice's pious couplet, 'He marks not that you won or lost, but how you played the game', at the same time as recognizing the importance of winning.

By the turn of the century society had changed, and so had cricket. Although King Edward VII did not accede until 1901, the style of his reign certainly preceded his kingship. His social importance as Prince of Wales and the differences between what he and his mother Queen Victoria represented were influential in the changing attitudes that were clearly recognizable during the 1890s. As for cricket, it was no longer a youthful and impressionable pastime with county and international competitions in their infancy, but established and secure. As such it was ideally poised to gain maximum benefit from developments outside the game that would so encourage its progress and elevate its position.

This was the period which witnessed the dramatic popularization of cricket, encouraged by certain key economic and social developments which took place during the latter decades of the nineteenth century. First was the spread of the railways to provide a national system of transport which not only linked the main centres of population but spread out like the tentacles of a great octopus into the provinces and remote rural areas. As well as being so extensive, the railways — at least third-class travel — proved to be affordable by most people.

Towards the end of the nineteenth century, if the upper classes were beginning to find themselves with so much time for leisure that within a few years some of them had sunk into a kind of torpor, the working classes were becoming accustomed to their first, limited, allotted periods of leisure and holiday. New legislation introduced during the 1870s meant that, for the first time, a shorter working week (around 55 hours) allowed for Saturday afternoons to be free and also introduced four Bank Holidays. On these occasions crowds turned up in their thousands to watch cricket, and the two summer Bank Holiday weekends — at Whitsun and in early August — became the traditional occasions for local Derbies between rivals or neighbours, most famously the 'Roses' match between Lancashire and Yorkshire. The two highest totals for attendances at a three-day first-class match in England still date from the Edwardian period. In 1906 over 80,000 packed into The Oval to watch Surrey play Yorkshire and in 1904 nearly 79,000 had attended the Roses match at Leeds. For the largest and most popular grounds of the major counties, annual attendances were regularly in excess of 200,000.

The standard 'gate' money was sixpence, and, in his biography of Gilbert Jessop, *The Croucher*, Gerald Brodribb describes an occasion at Hastings in 1899 when the well-known umpire Bob Thoms was determined that the 'sixpennies' would not miss their entertainment. Jessop was batting and was clearly out stumped when, to the general astonishment of fielders and batsman alike, Thoms called 'not out' from square leg. Coming in to replace the bails he explained his decision. 'Sixpenny crowd — Saturday gate — can't disappoint 'em — near thing, near thing — but not near enough for the occasion.'

Such popularity had an immediate and beneficial effect upon the finances of county clubs, which were also boosted by swelling memberships, rising in some cases from a few hundred to over two thousand. Given the hugely increased numbers that the major grounds were now having to accommodate, most counties celebrated cricket's emergence as a national spectator sport with extensive improvements to their grounds. Not surprisingly the example was set by the grandest and wealthiest club, the MCC, whose new pavilion at Lord's was built in time for the 1890 season and ranks as a

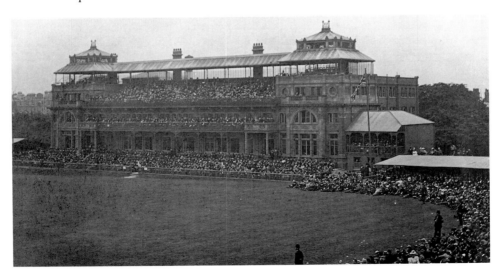

Cricket's greatest monument, the Lord's pavilion, completed in 1890 and here filled to capacity during the 1896 England v. Australia Test.

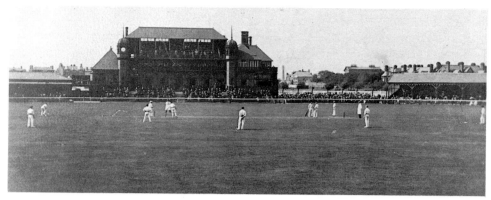

*Old Trafford's new pavilion, opened in 1895, an architectural assertion of
Edwardian confidence in cricket.*

supreme example of *fin de siècle* architecture. The counties may not have been able to
afford such splendour but they followed suit, and happily most of their efforts survive
today. There is no question that virtually all the county pavilions with any architectural
merit or character were built during this period: Old Trafford in 1895, The Oval in 1896
(these two designed by the same architect), Scarborough 1895, Chesterfield 1898,
Worcester 1899, Canterbury 1900, Bournemouth 1902 and Maidstone 1910. Many
county committees were also keen to take advantage of any non-cricketing income their
fine new buildings might have enabled them to attract. At Trent Bridge, ladies' dancing
classes appear to have been something of a speciality: in 1902 Miss Stanhope's class paid
£7 10s., in 1905 Mrs Munro's paid £8 11s. Another regular user was the St Saviour's Boys
Brigade, while in 1905 there was a Lady Day Church Bazaar and a private party thrown by
a Mr J. Morris.

As the first-class game was organized into a proper championship with enough
counties involved to be nationally representative and to take cricket to virtually all of
England's largest cities and many other major towns, so the example was followed at all
levels, and the heroes of the day were emulated by scores of admirers and disciples. In an
essay on sport which appeared in *Edwardian England* published in 1964, John Arlott
concluded that, 'the game's real health and strength lay in its local roots. Not a town or
village but had its club, while churches, institutes, schools, factories, collieries, and the
most fortuitous groupings of young men had their teams. Never, before or since, were
there so many active cricketers in England.'

In the north the majority of the leagues who have dominated the game in these
counties ever since were founded: the Lancashire League in 1890, the Central Lancashire
League in 1891, the Bradford League in 1903. Once established they produced a
competitive high standard of cricket and a constant supply of players for Lancashire and
Yorkshire. In the south this was at once the real blossoming and the hey-day of club
cricket, both for resident clubs, and the wandering clubs of amateurs who ranged from
the socially élite I Zingari to more modest bands whose annual fixture list might be

Hampstead CC, one of the strongest in the country, celebrated each season with
lavish annual dinners and were justifiably proud of their vice-president, the
Australian 'Demon' of the 1880s, F.R. Spofforth.

limited to a late-summer tour to a favourite cricketing part of the country. The services became another stronghold, with the first representative match between the Army and the Navy being played at Lord's in 1908 and given first-class status, and more officers having the time and talent to play first-class cricket for counties than has ever been the case since.

Consciousness of cricket was fostered by coverage in the press, and in particular by the emergence of popular newspapers heralded by the *Daily Mail*, first printed in 1896. The *Daily Express* followed in 1901 and the *Daily Mirror* in 1904. County cricket and other first-class games were covered exhaustively and the style was usually more lively than the dusty factual material which appeared in the columns of the established qualities such as *The Times* and *Morning Post*. For those who could afford it there was the new weekly journal *Cricket*, founded by Charles Alcock, Surrey's entrepreneurial secretary at The Oval, while on an altogether more robust level there was the most popular of the new halfpenny weeklies, *Ally Sloper's Half Holiday*, in which the hideous hero – adored by thousands of the working class – and his friends always attended or were involved in the major matches of the season.

The popularization of cricket, its attendance by thousands and its newsworthiness to the papers resulted in the game's leading players becoming national figures. This in itself was a new phenomenon because previously no sportsman had enjoyed any sort of reputation outside the players and followers of his particular sport, with one major exception: W.G. Grace. As we shall see, Grace opened our period with a quite staggering revival of his batting at a time when most people presumed that he was in a gentle but inevitable decline. By so doing he confirmed that if he was not 'the best known man in England', to coin a well-used description, the only rivals he had for the position were the Prince of Wales and Mr Gladstone. By a combination of the manner in which he personally revolutionized cricket over a period of four decades, his physical appearance and his personality, Grace acquired a status which no other cricketer has ever been able to rival. But in so doing he demonstrated the heights of popular awareness and acclaim that it was now possible for sportsmen to reach, and paved the way for his successors by ensuring that their deeds would be judged beyond the confines of the game.

Despite reaching the zenith of his fame during the Edwardian era, Grace remained firmly representative of the Victorian age into which he was born. His cricketing technique and achievements set the standards for all who followed, but his boisterousness belonged to the more rugged period of the game's development which had gone before. He had too many rough edges, a lack of worldliness and little regard for social niceties or appearances, all of which were to be ironed out in the debonair elegance of Edwardianism personified by men such as The Hon. Stanley Jackson. When Grace's son – also W.G. – played for Cambridge in the University Match in 1895, the first of his two appearances, the Old Man proudly bought his first silk top hat and frock coat for the occasion, prompting the quip from a friend that he would not be recognized.

Grace's career awakened in cricket a cult of personality, the sporting idol, which was to become a hallmark of the Edwardian period. It was one of the anomalies of the age that, while conformity was expected, individualism among the successful was greatly enjoyed and, in such cases, quirks of character or behaviour were easily forgiven.

Writing in 1930, Neville Cardus went so far as to argue that, 'Between 1890 and 1914 the history of English cricket can only be discussed in terms of Men, each a character and law unto himself, each playing the game in a way vividly his own.'

In the same vein, Colonel Philip Trevor maintained that at any time between 1897 when he began seriously watching first-class cricket and 1914, he had no need of a scorecard or scoreboard to identify a batsman, he could recognize them from their methods. If his assertions were partially prompted by his dissatisfaction with cricket at the time he was writing (1921), such individuality was the essence of the Edwardian game. It was largely assisted by the attitude, prevalent at least among the amateurs if not the professionals whose livelihoods depended upon their performances, that the amassing of runs was not the all-important *raison d'être* for batting. Equally if not more important was the manner in which runs were scored, so that they preferred to make an elegant or exciting 30 runs than a long and grafting century.

Whether revelling in their self-appointed roles as entertainers or preferring more modestly to express and improve upon their natural ability, they played cricket for pleasure, and herein lay the secret of their appeal. The nonchalance and apparent effortlessness which they displayed expressed the apparent ability to excel without trying which has been seen as typically English but which was most apposite during this period. In most cases the foundation of their success was far more hard work than may have seemed the case, and the assimilation of great technical knowledge about the game which a number of them, Ranjitsinhji, C.B. Fry and Archie MacLaren to name three, were to demonstrate in instructive books about cricket.

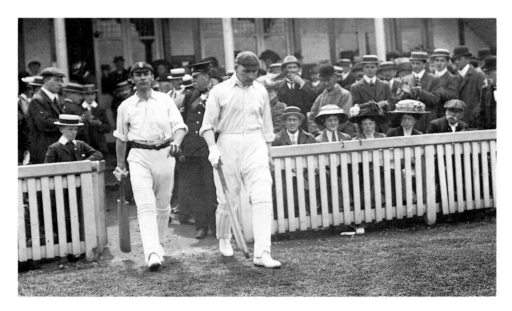

England's captain Archie MacLaren (right) walks out with Jack Hobbs to open the innings against Australia at Edgbaston in 1909.

Such lionizing of the amateurs is not in any way to belittle the contribution of the professionals, and it was a select group of professionals: Arthur Shrewsbury and George Gunn, J.T. Tyldesley, Tom Hayward and Jack Hobbs, Wilfred Rhodes, George Hirst and Sydney Barnes, who, by the mastery they displayed over one or more departments of batting or bowling, made the most telling long-term contributions to cricket's development. But the Edwardian period witnessed the great flowering of amateurism in English sport in general and cricket in particular. Never again would amateurs be able to afford to play cricket in anything more than small numbers and usually on an irregular basis. Given these limitations very few were ever able to compete with the professionals at the highest levels.

It was the amateur contribution to Edwardian cricket which gave the game its period flavour. They played cricket because they had the time and the resources, because they enjoyed it and were good at it and because, as Neville Cardus pointed out, from the 1890s it was unrivalled among sports as a socially acceptable pastime:

> In the '90s cricket was looked upon as the gentleman's game; tennis was not yet popular with men of proper late-Victorian masculinity; it was a game for what was then known as the 'masher', with his straw boater and his designs on the 'fair sex'. Golf was more for the middle-aged; while football was deemed mainly 'low' unless it was possible to play for the Corinthians.

As many of them did, for while cricket may have been the most socially acceptable pastime this was the period when sport in general was celebrated in an unprecedented manner and, as John Arlott wrote, 'all-rounders were to be found in greater profusion in Edwardian times than at any other.' Young men leaving Oxford or Cambridge with more than one 'blue' were commonplace, although no one rivalled C.B. Fry in his extraordinary range of achievement. A triple blue at Oxford (cricket, association football and athletics) – during which time he set the world long-jump record – he missed his rugby football blue through injury. After leaving Oxford, as well as his cricket for Sussex, the Gentlemen and England, he played football for the Corinthians, in the FA Cup, and for England – and rugby for the Barbarians. These were only the organized sports in which he attained the highest levels; at most others he was more than proficient.

Fry was the exception, but for many other amateurs a summer's cricket was often followed by a winter playing either football – most of them for the Corinthians, whose sides were picked from the public school old boys' clubs – or rugby. The best footballer who also played first-class cricket was G.O. Smith, while other leading Corinthians were the elegant Somerset batsman Lionel Palairet, and the Kent batsman S.H. Day. R.E. Foster was the most dazzling member of the gifted Worcestershire brotherhood (seven in all) and the only man in history to captain England at both cricket and football. One brother (G.N.) also played first-class cricket and football for England while another (H.K.) captained Worcestershire and was the English amateur rackets champion.

The best rugby player among county cricketers was Somerset's captain Sammy Woods who got his blue for both sports at Cambridge and later played rugby for Somerset and England, as well as football for Sussex. The neatest was the incomparable Lancashire

Worcester 1905. H.K. Foster (right), the county's captain and all-round sportsman, with the diminutive Australian Syd Gregory who made eight tours to England.

batsman Reggie Spooner, who played rugby for his home club Liverpool and for England. Built in a very different mould to the delicate Spooner was the Essex and England cricket captain Johnny Douglas, who won an Olympic gold medal as a middleweight boxer in 1908 and played football as an amateur for England.

The desire to excel as an all-rounder, the public admiration for such ability and the combination of manliness and skill which it represented were intrinsic to the Edwardian ethos. Sporting brilliance for some people took on an aesthetic quality, while underlying the surging developments was a nationalistic vigour born of the self-confidence, at times complacency, of the average Edwardian Englishman. England was to them the place where sport was being fostered in the supreme manner, and international competitions which were to rise to pre-eminence between the wars were still only of peripheral importance. The Olympic Games were in their infancy and, after their revival at Athens in 1896, it was entirely appropriate that the first genuinely successful Games were held at London in 1908. The most established and evenly fought competitions were England v. Australia Test matches. All this bred a sense of superiority which, during the two decades that it lasted until shattered by the horrors of the First World War, characterized the sporting Edwardians and their attitude to life.

2

THE DAWN OF MODERN CRICKET

The twenty seasons between 1895 and the outbreak of the First World War witnessed the organization of cricket as it has been known – with few fundamental changes – ever since. This organization took place throughout the period and in different areas: in the administration of both English and international cricket and the laws that controlled them, in batting and bowling styles and the wickets that were played on. As a result, while the English game in 1914 was clearly different to that of the 1880s, it was very similar to that of the 1930s and later years.

As far as the domestic first-class game was concerned the most important changes came at the beginning of the period when the county championship was extended to embrace more counties and was organized under the auspices of the MCC. The 1895 season witnessed county cricket being played for the first time within the framework of a well-organized and representative competition and it is from that date that most records of the championship have run.

At the beginning of the 1890s the counties themselves had set up the County Cricket Council to attempt to establish a viable framework for first-class and lesser county games. The scheme was a failure through disagreement, for the county representatives were to a man forthright and fiercely defensive of their own county's interests. In 1891, after a short and ineffective life, the council was voted into extinction by its own members.

At the time, the first-class counties consisted of the 'big eight': Yorkshire, Lancashire, Nottinghamshire, Kent, Middlesex, Surrey, Sussex and Gloucestershire. Somerset were allowed to join the fold for the 1891 season and the West Countrymen promptly silenced the sceptics by defeating the champions, Surrey. Otherwise no real progress was made until the autumn of 1894 when delegates from the counties met at Lord's. Yorkshire proposed that, 'For the purposes of classification there should be no distinction drawn between counties who play out and home three-day matches with not less than six other counties.' Again there was disagreement, but this time the counties decided upon a positive step and went to arbitration. They requested the MCC to consider and pass judgement upon the vexed question.

As a result acknowledged authority was vested in the MCC. Considering that they were viewed as suitably expert, eminent and impartial, that the club already controlled the Laws of the game and owned the most prestigious ground, it was most likely that their authority would grow in future years, as indeed it did. Their response to the

The county captains at Lord's in 1901. Standing: D.L.A. Jephson (Surrey),
G.L. Jessop (Glos), R.E. Foster (Worcestershire), S.M.J. Woods (Somerset),
J.R. Mason (Kent); seated: G. MacGregor (Middlesex), H.W. Bainbridge (Warwicks),
H.G. Owen (Essex), Lord Hawke (Yorkshire), C.E. de Trafford (Leics).

counties' overture was decisive. In October 1894 they announced a scheme which would
take effect from the beginning of the next season.

> Cricketing counties shall be considered as belonging to the first-class or not. There is
> no necessity for any further subdivision. First-class counties are those whose matches
> with one another, with the MCC and Ground, with the Universities, with the
> Australians and other such Elevens as shall be adjudged 'first-class matches' by the
> MCC Committee, are used in compilation of first-class batting and bowling averages.
> There shall be no limit to the number of first-class counties. The MCC Committee
> may bring new counties into the list, may remove existing ones from it, or may do
> both. The list for 1895 is as follows: Derbyshire, Essex, Gloucestershire, Hampshire,
> Kent, Lancashire, Leicestershire, Middlesex, Nottinghamshire, Somersetshire, Sur-
> rey, Sussex, Warwickshire, Yorkshire.
> After the close of each cricket season the Committee of the MCC shall decide the
> County Championship. It shall be competed for by first-class counties. No county shall
> be eligible unless it shall have played at least eight out-and-home matches with other
> counties; provided that if no play can take place owing to weather or other

unavoidable causes, such match shall be reckoned as unfinished. One point shall be reckoned for each win; one point shall be deducted for each loss; unfinished games shall not be reckoned. The county which, during the season, shall have, in finished matches, obtained the greatest proportionate number of points shall be reckoned the Champion county.

And so, in this succinct yet weighty pronouncement, the MCC outlined a competition that was to run under its auspices until the formation of the Test and County Cricket Board over 70 years later and which has only changed in detail, such as the number of points allotted and the number of games played. They welcomed five new counties: Derbyshire (readmitted, having dropped out in 1887), Essex, Hampshire, Leicestershire and Warwickshire, making the total 14. With the addition of Worcestershire in 1899 and Northamptonshire in 1905, the championship was played for the rest of the period with only one county fewer than the current number, which was made up soon after the First World War with the addition of Glamorgan in 1921.

The effect was dramatic and far-reaching. With a competition that was both broad-based and clearly organized, county cricket attained an importance during the domestic season second only to that of Test matches against Australia – and there were some who felt that it should take pride of place over these. At the same time the first-class game was offered to new and wider audiences just at the time when demand was growing rapidly. It could not have come at a better time, both for cricket and for the English public, and the success was borne out throughout the period both by the standard of play and its popularity.

As the MCC were invited by the counties to assume authority over the domestic first-class game, so they were asked to do the same regarding Test cricket. The organization of Test matches had begun to be widely viewed as unsatisfactory mainly because the regular three Tests were always played on the same grounds: Lord's, The Oval and Old Trafford. This meant that not only did the host committee – the MCC, Surrey and Lancashire respectively – have sole responsibility for choosing the England side for their match, but they were also the only ones who benefited either financially or from the accompanying prestige.

There were occasions when other county committees put self-interest before patriotism and refused to release players for Test matches, notably Yorkshire, captained by Lord Hawke, who felt no urge to respond when no Test matches were played in Yorkshire. There were also felt to be regular inconsistencies in the selection process, most notoriously in 1896 when the MCC left Ranjitsinhji out of the First Test; in Lord Harris's immortal phrase he was 'a bird of passage'.

In 1895 an impetus for change was provided by the Australians, who were looking ahead to their proposed tour of 1896. At the time of Britain's imperial zenith and as a result possibly sensitive about any condescension from the old country, despite their proven ability to compete at cricket on equal terms, they made it clear that they would like an official invitation from an official host – as was the case when English sides went to Australia – and that they would like to play five Tests. Although there was a partial response to the first part of their request when the MCC joined with the counties in

HEADS AND TAILS.—FIRST MATCH.

The Lion.—"YAH! WHAT A TAIL!"
The Kangaroo.—"YES, LEO; BUT I CAN PUT A HEAD ON YOU."

*A Melbourne cartoonist's idea of Australia's likely success during their tour of
1896.*

*Lord Hawke, captain of Yorkshire for nearly thirty years, here giving fielding
practice in front of the Bramall Lane pavilion.*

extending the warmest possible welcome, the move for five Test matches cut little ice at
the county secretaries' 1895 end-of-season meeting at Lord's. Only one county
supported the suggestion.

It was not until 1898, with the prospect of another Australian visit in 1899, that
change came about. Lord Hawke confirmed that his lack of enthusiasm to release
Yorkshire players for Tests was prompted by dissatisfaction that no Tests were played in
Yorkshire, when he made a decisive speech in May 1898, calling for the formation of a
board of control. At the subsequent county meeting a resolution was passed that again
looked to the MCC. It requested that:

> The MCC should appoint a Board to govern future Test matches between England and
> Australia at home. It was afterwards agreed, 'that such Board be composed of the
> President of MCC, five of his club committee, and one representative from six of the

first-class counties selected by the MCC to send a representative. The President of the MCC to have the casting vote.'

It was the clearest acknowledgement possible of the esteem in which the MCC was held. Indeed, it is unlikely that the club has ever again been offered so flattering a gesture. Not only were they asked to take the lead, they were offered the controlling interest in the regulation of Test cricket in this country. It was a natural corollary that they should assume responsibility for English tours abroad, which they did a few years later with the 1903–04 tour to Australia.

The new Board of Control met for the first time at the end of 1898. They announced that for the Australian visit of 1899 five Tests would be played, at the three current grounds, at Nottingham and, inevitably, in Yorkshire. At the same time they announced that the selection of English sides would be left to a committee of three men, the first three being W.G. Grace, Lord Hawke himself and H.W. Bainbridge, the captain of Warwickshire who had been a friend of Lord Hawke at Eton and Cambridge, but otherwise seemed a surprising choice for the position.

As far as the laws which controlled matches were concerned, there were two areas in particular, the follow-on and declarations, where the regulations needed changing, as was demonstrated by some fairly notorious and stormy episodes during the mid-1890s. Curiously enough – or perhaps not so, considering their prestige and cachet – the two matches which questioned the follow-on law in the most publicized circumstances were both between Oxford and Cambridge at Lord's, the University Matches of 1893 and 1896.

A scene from the controversial University Match of 1896. Three of the Oxford side, J.C. Hartley, G.R. Bardswell and P.F. Warner, leaving the field.

In 1893 the law stated that the follow-on was compulsory if the side batting second was 80 runs or more behind. Cambridge had scored 182 and Oxford were 95 for nine wickets when they decided that their best chance of victory lay in taking advantage of the compulsory follow-on, batting again and gaining a lead, then bowling Cambridge out on a breaking wicket. Therefore in an attempt to avoid scoring the seven runs which would have saved the follow-on and allowed Cambridge to bat, they clearly attempted to throw away the last wicket.

Their intended tactics may not have been in the best spirit of the game, but the Cambridge captain F.S. Jackson, and his bowler C.M. Wells, proved that they were more than a match for such skulduggery. A combination of deliberately unplayable no-balls and wides to the boundary ensured that Oxford accrued the vital runs and Cambridge were able to bat again. The significance of the situation was borne out when Cambridge went on to win by 266 runs, but such blatant gamesmanship did not endear the young undergraduates to either the authorities at Lord's or the spectators.

In 1896, by which time the deficit had been extended to 120 runs but the follow-on was still compulsory, events at the University Match were sensational and a decisive influence on the significant change in the law which came a few years later. Once again it was Cambridge who employed the questionable tactics, having batted first and scored 319. During Oxford's first innings the Cambridge captain, Frank Mitchell, had already aroused some spectators by ordering Gilbert Jessop to bowl aggressive bouncers, which not only resulted in injuries to the Oxford batsmen but in one instance to the Cambridge wicket-keeper as well. Then, with Oxford ten runs short of saving the follow-on, Mitchell ensured that they would not have the chance of batting again immediately by ordering E.B. Shine to bowl no-balls to the boundary until the ten runs had been scored.

In the already heated atmosphere it was too much for many spectators who, immediately they saw what the Cambridge captain was up to, began barracking vociferously. A few minutes later, Oxford having only saved the follow-on by three runs before being all out, the Cambridge side returned to the pavilion to a distinctly hostile reception. Mitchell himself gained a blue at rugby and putting the shot, as well as cricket, and was not easily intimidated, but he afterwards maintained that he was certainly nervous when one elderly and enraged MCC member hurled his binoculars at him. According to Gerald Brodribb in his biography of Jessop, another MCC stalwart stood in the path of the Cambridge side as they filed into the pavilion, but he was so apoplectic with rage that, 'as he tried to find words he just made clucking noises. Hemingway, one of the Cambridge side who also played for Gloucester, said to him. "I'll have that one for breakfast, sir, when you've laid it." '

In the end Mitchell's tactics came to naught and Oxford pulled off an unlikely and spectacular win by four wickets. Discussion of the match even made a leading article in *The Times*, the paper thundering on about 'deploring the actions' and 'degenerating into competitiveness' in characteristically trenchant tones. But the most important outcome came in 1900 when, in an overall review of the Laws by the MCC, it was announced that the deficit for a follow-on would be 150 runs (for a three-day match) and that enforcement by the fielding side was *optional* – the vital alteration. The law has since remained unchanged.

A second significant alteration during the 1900 review of the Laws was made regarding declarations. The late 1890s and early 1900s witnessed an unprecedented series of enormous innings totals amassed in first-class matches: between 1895 and 1900 there were 21 of 600 and over (including three totals of 800 and over) and between 1900 and 1910 a total of 33 of 600 and over. The significance of so many enormous scores within 15 years is put into perspective by the fact that they represent nearly 40 per cent of the totals of 600 and over attained in England during the 170 years between 1815 and 1985.

The main cause of these huge scores was the law which, until 1900, did not allow a declaration until the last day of a three-day match. As a result the situation often arose that the side batting first had amassed so many runs and batted for so much time that a result was impossible, and therefore they opted to bat on in pursuit of a large total. In 1900 the first step towards making declarations more realistic was taken when the law was amended so that a side could declare at any time from lunch on the second day. As the continuation of enormous scores bore out, however, this was fairly ineffectual and in 1910 another alteration allowed a declaration at any time on the second day.

One immediate result, which has been the case ever since, was that the opportunity and timing of a declaration began to assume tactical importance. In 1900 Derbyshire tried to declare their second innings against Essex without even starting it, but the veteran umpire Alfred Shaw, who had played nearly all his cricket when there was no declaration law at all, was having none of it and sent them in. He was supported by the MCC. Derbyshire stayed only until a wicket had fallen for no runs and then declared. This situation eventually led to the addition of a clause giving permission for a captain to forfeit his second innings.

Perhaps more significant was the first occasion when a captain batting second won a match, having declared his first innings closed before overhauling his opponents' score, as Hampshire achieved against Northamptonshire in 1908. A similarly tactical situation had occurred the previous season when Gloucestershire took advantage of the 1900 law to declare twice in one day in an attempt to beat their Somerset neighbours.

If there were two sides to the argument about amending both the follow-on and declaration laws the great majority of people were agreed that change was badly needed. No such clear-cut approval existed over the contentious issue of lbw which went through one of the stormier episodes in its evolution around the turn of the century. At the time the lbw law, which had stood since the eighteenth century, stated that the ball had to pitch straight *and* that the leg – or other part of the body struck – had also to be in line with the wicket.

A strong movement for reform was prompted by two developments during the late 1890s: first, the clear superiority enjoyed by batsmen over bowlers, and the quantity of drawn matches which this produced, and second, the growing – if highly criticized – practice for skilful batsmen to use their pads as a second line of defence. Arthur Shrewsbury of Nottinghamshire was usually cited as the chief protagonist of this tactic which – probably unfairly – was regarded as illustrative of dour professionalism. The would-be reformers had a redoubtable leader in the figure of The Hon. Alfred Lyttelton, Cambridge and England cricketer, politician, President of the MCC in 1898 and a member of the MCC committee. They proposed that a batsman could be out if the ball pitched outside the line of the stumps so long as the impact was made on line. The issue came to a head at the MCC annual meeting of 1901. In the event the motion for change was carried but failed to secure the necessary two-thirds majority and so the law remained unchanged – until 1937. But the debate was a clear harbinger of the manner in which potentially contentious technical points of play and issues in the Laws would play a part in the evolution of the modern game.

If bowlers often felt the odds to be weighted in favour of batsmen, one issue that cast a cloud over their claims during the years leading up to the turn of the century was the widespread suspicion of and regular blatant examples of illegal actions or throwing. Despite being led by no less a figure than Lord Harris, without question the single most authoritative and powerful figure in the game, the campaign against throwing made little progress for years, largely because of an understandable reluctance on the part of umpires – all of whom were ex-professionals – to take steps which would almost inevitably end the career of a worthy professional bowler.

The lead came from a somewhat unexpected quarter, a South Australian called Jim Phillips, who came to England and played for Middlesex and later umpired in both countries. He first caused a ripple during A.E. Stoddart's 1897–98 tour to Australia, when he no-balled the Australian bowler Ernest Jones for throwing – a brave thing for any umpire to do to an Australian in a home Test. Back in England in 1898 he continued his campaign, most notably when he no-balled C.B. Fry. Amateurs did not expect this sort of treatment and, not surprisingly, the self-opinionated Fry was highly aggrieved and

Jim Phillips (left), the umpire who led an unrelenting campaign against bowlers with illegal actions, and his ardent supporter, Sydney Pardon, editor of Wisden *and probably the most authoritative commentator of the period.*

protested his innocence. Sydney Pardon, the forthright editor of *Wisden*, who had himself for many years waged a written war against the offenders, had no hesitation in writing that it was a case of 'long-delayed justice'.

At last, at the end of the 1900 season, the county captains finally bit the bullet and announced that they would not include in their sides any bowler suspected of having an illegal action. Such fine principle may not have been put into action so readily had not Jim Phillips inflicted the *coup de grâce* in 1901. Umpiring a match between Lancashire and Somerset at Old Trafford he 'called' the Lancashire and England bowler Arthur Mold 16 times in ten overs. This relentless condemnation of such a successful and established bowler would admittedly have been more moderate if Mold had been taken off earlier by Lancashire's captain Archie MacLaren, not known for a liking of being brow-beaten. But in the circumstances it was decisive, and throwing was not to be a real problem in first-class cricket for another fifty years. Poor Mold's career was over, but many people agreed with Sydney Pardon who predictably concluded: 'I regard Mold as the luckiest of men to have gone through a dozen seasons before being no-balled.' Even when Mold died twenty years later Pardon could not resist driving the final proverbial nail in his coffin when he ended his *Wisden* obituary with the words, 'He did wonders for Lancashire but personally I always thought he was in a false position.'

Neville Cardus wrote in *English Cricket*, published in 1945:

> The years from 1890 to 1914 witnessed the Golden Age of batsmanship. Years of sowing were now reaped: the technique was now ready for cultured use. The stage was at last prepared; and the producer was the groundsman and his roller. A great batsman could now on fine days give his mind to the display of his arts, confident that he need only solve the known problems of his material – in other words the bowling opposed to him, which could be studied in the abstract as well as in fact, free of incalculable and unscientific misconduct caused by a rough and entirely unscientific pitch. The groundsman, the producer or stage manager of cricket, made the mistake of producers in the theatre – he became engrossed in the spectacle and the setting at the expense of the play. He made the conditions in which a virtuoso display of skill was positively encouraged; the great batsman could absorb himself in the perfection of his own art in the face of an attack largely reduced to a static mechanism. But there was scope also for the virtuoso bowler – for none except the inspired artist of pace or spin or flight could hope on a perfect pitch to emerge from a perspiring anonymity. The circumstances so much favoured batsmanship that the technique of stroke-play and footwork developed at a pace which outran and outwitted every bowler not of the highest class.

In characteristic language Cardus perhaps overstresses the hopelessness of the bowlers' cause and romanticizes the role of the groundsman, but he does highlight the improvement of wickets which took place during the period. Specifically this was the result of the widespread introduction of marl which had first been used during the 1880s by 'Fiddler' Walker in Nottinghamshire. The flawless Trent Bridge wickets became renowned for their encouragement to batsmen, and by the mid-1890s groundsmen at most of the major county grounds were following Walker's example, the most famous of whom were Sam Apted at The Oval and Fred Hunt at Worcester.

The smooth mixture produced by marl, except in unusually wet conditions, went a long way towards guaranteeing a predictable playing surface, but equally important were more general technical improvements in groundsmanship. These were brought about by a combination of late-nineteenth-century developments such as better grass-seeds and machinery and a general willingness among the county clubs for their groundsmen to be well equipped. Together they ensured that not only were wickets well prepared but also, with more efficient and regular rolling and mowing, outfields were smoother.

The end-of-year accounts of all the county clubs carried entries similar to those for 1905 in the Trent Bridge ground account, the details of which included:

	£	s.	d.
Groundsman wages:	65	12	00
Man assisting:	11	5	4
Youth assisting:	13	1	0
Keep of horse:	3	5	0
Hire of horse:	2	13	0
Corn for horse:	11	18	5
Repairing horse boots:	3	14	11
Rolling and mowing ground:	2	16	6
Turf for ground:	4	19	8
Clay for ground:	3	6	2
Repairing lawnmower, etc:	5	6	0

Encouraged by a feeling of relative security regarding the playing surface – certainly compared to what their predecessors during the middle and latter decades of the nineteenth century had had to endure – batsmen were able to concentrate on the task of getting the better of the bowling. Although it is difficult to generalize upon the improvements in batting style and technique, there is no doubt that the man whose attitude towards bowling was central to the developments of the period was W.G. Grace. The manner in which he batted notwithstanding, for no batsman can realistically be copied by another with any hope of success, Grace demonstrated certain principles of batting, most notably with his watchword, 'get at the bowler before he gets at you', with the fact that he played each ball on its individual merit, and his mastery of both forward and back play. As a result he was able to dominate bowling in a manner which had never been achieved before, especially perhaps in the manner in which he attacked fast bowling, and in so doing set an example to his successors.

For many batsmen of the period, in particular the amateurs, it was the manner in which they scored their runs rather than the scores they amassed which they felt to be of primary importance. All the same, the ability to run up large scores gained important encouragement from a change in the Laws in 1910. Up to that date a six was only awarded for a hit which actually carried out of the ground; now it would count for any

*The Champion: W.G. Grace towards the end of his career, sitting between his
two sons W.G. junior (left) and C.B.*

hit clearing the boundary, which had previously only been awarded four. This has remained the law ever since. In addition to the quantities of enormous innings totals and individual scores, the run-scoring of the period is emphatically demonstrated by partnership records. With the exception of the second wicket, for no one managed to overhaul the 398 made by Nottinghamshire's Arthur Shrewsbury and William Gunn in 1890, the period saw a new partnership record set for each wicket. Of these, six have never been passed in England and two have been overtaken just once.

Bowling may have been hard work in the circumstances, but, partly as a result of the greater need for ingenuity and skill as pointed out by Cardus, it reached great heights. It was during this period that the repertoire of bowling as it has been known ever since was completed with the addition of two decisive new methods of attack: swing bowling and the googly.

When a change in the law came in 1900, extending the number of balls in an over from five to the modern total of six, optimistic bowlers may have felt that it gave them an extra chance to get at the batsmen. The less self-assured felt it to be another opportunity for the batsman to score runs. Other than the privileged minority of brilliant bowlers, whether fast like Tom Richardson, medium-paced like Sydney Barnes and George Hirst, or slow like Charlie Blythe and Wilfred Rhodes, who could reckon to threaten most batsmen, wickets were gained by grafting away, over after over, planning a batsman's downfall in the manner that Cardus described the Australian George Giffen planning Arthur Shrewsbury's:

Giffen would set himself at twelve o'clock to get Arthur Shrewsbury out at 4.15

precisely, by the means of a far-seeing plan of varied balls, the crucial one to be delivered after a tireless succession of others which had never once suggested that the 'trick-card' was in Giffen's hand at all.

English cricketers got an inkling of the possibilities of 'swerve' bowling from an unlikely quarter in 1897, when the Gentlemen of Philadelphia first visited England. One of their team was John Barton King who, over the next ten years, was to prove himself a world-class bowler with the ability to clearly move the ball in the air, which many people presumed he learnt from baseball pitchers. Among English bowlers it was the Yorkshireman, George Hirst, who first perfected the art of swing bowling, or 'swerve' as it was then called. Looking for means of advancing from predictable bowling – however hostile or clever – bowlers began to appreciate the potential of moving the ball through the air, as well as using the seam for movement off the wicket. The significance of these advances was confirmed in 1907 with the passing of the new-ball law in 1907, allowing for a new ball after a side had scored 200 runs.

As important and if anything more ingenious was the introduction of the googly, first demonstrated by the amateur B.J.T. Bosanquet. Many years after he had retired from playing cricket, when the impact of the googly had been constantly discussed, he himself described how he evolved his 'invention':

> Somewhere about the year 1897 [the year before he went up to Oxford] I was playing a game with a tennis ball, known as 'Twisti-Twosti'. The object was to bounce the ball on a table so that your opponent sitting opposite could not catch it . . . After a little experimenting I managed to pitch the ball which broke in a certain direction; then with more or less the same delivery make the next ball go in the opposite direction! I practised the same thing with a soft ball at 'stump-cricket'. From this I progressed to the cricket ball . . . I devoted a great deal of time to practising the googly in the nets, occasionally in unimportant matches. The first public recognition was obtained in July 1900, for Middlesex v. Leicestershire at Lord's. An unfortunate individual [Coe, the left-hander] had made 98 when he was stumped off a fine specimen which bounced four times . . . This small beginning marked the start of what came to be termed a revolution in bowling.

Although Bosanquet's full-time career – like so many amateurs – was confined to only a few seasons with Middlesex after he left Oxford, he perfected his discovery very quickly. By the time that he visited Australia for the first time, as a member of Lord Hawke's side in 1902–03, he had the measure of the best batsmen anywhere, as he showed with a delivery to Trumper who had made 40 'in about 20 minutes. Two leg-breaks were played beautifully to cover, but the next ball (delivered with a silent prayer) pitched in the same place, saw the same graceful stroke played – and struck the middle stump instead of the bat!' In Australia the googly is still called the Bosie.

Advances in the techniques of batting and bowling were accompanied by a clearly discernible improvement in the general standard of fielding, assisted by the better mown and smoother outfields. As well as a response to the quality of the batsmen, it reflected,

*B.J.T. Bosanquet, as an undergraduate at Oxford
where he perfected the 'googly', his new delivery.*

first, the increased competitiveness of county games and, second, the strategic advances of bowlers who bowled to a tightly set field and did not expect the batsmen to be allowed to escape a well-planned trap by lapses or dropped catches. Specialist slip fielders, such as Yorkshire's John Tunnicliffe, Kent's Frank Woolley and the Nottinghamshire captain A.O. Jones, constantly rewarded their side's fast bowlers, while elsewhere, especially at cover, the speed and reliability of such men as Gloucestershire's Gilbert Jessop, Lancashire's Reggie Spooner and Surrey's Jack Hobbs, were perfected in order to counter the batsmen's favourite shots.

The various improvements reflected the extent to which cricket was becoming a thinking game as well as an active one, as players strove to attain technical perfection in one department or another. Of course this was to a great extent prompted by the desire to win, but it was equally a product of the desire to master the game as a science which had not been widely evident before. For the first time books discussing the technical aspects of the game began to be published regularly, while the major issues and contentions of the time and the style and form of individual players was discussed exhaustively in the annual editions of *Wisden* under the control of Sydney Pardon, the editor from 1891 to 1925. Pardon became one of the most influential observers and commentators in the game's history, and single-handedly established the unrivalled prestige of *Wisden*. The success of the annual almanack was as good an indication as any off-the-field development that cricket had outgrown its somewhat rough-and-ready image and haphazard organization of the nineteenth century and become the modern game that, after this initial period of vigorous progress and expansion, was to evolve steadily throughout the twentieth century.

3

1895

As if to celebrate the reorganization and expansion of the county championship, the season of 1895 turned out to be one of the most memorable in history, with record-breaking performances by four individuals: W.G. Grace who became both the first batsman to score 100 hundreds, and the first to score 1,000 runs in May; C.L. Townsend who, aged 18, took 94 wickets in the month of August and ended the season top of the national bowling averages; Tom Richardson who took 290 wickets in the season; and finally A.C. MacLaren who scored 424 for Lancashire against Somerset, which remains the highest first-class score in England.

The home season was preceded by the ideal introduction: by winning the Fifth and final Test of the winter tour at Melbourne, A.E. Stoddart's England side clinched a marvellous series against Australia by three victories to two. With the Ashes secure, English cricketers were able to concentrate on affairs at home, and with no overseas tourists during the 1895 summer there was no distraction from the domestic programme.

On 9 March, three days after the victory in Melbourne and some weeks before the triumphal return of Stoddart and his team, there was an arrival at Dover of considerable significance for English cricket. Lord Harris returned to England after spending five years in India as Governor of Bombay. Within no time at all his lordship had gathered up the reins of Kent cricket and on 1 May he was appointed President of the MCC for the forthcoming year. Before his departure for India he had already established himself as one of the game's foremost figures and he had ruled over his county's cricket ever since assuming the captaincy at the age of 24. Although the presidency of the MCC throughout the late Victorian and Edwardian period was effectively an aristocratic sinecure demanding neither cricketing prowess nor involvement in the game, Lord Harris was an exception to the rule and his appointment confirmed his elevation to a position of unrivalled and largely unquestioned authority over the national game which he retained until his death in 1933.

Such was the power that Lord Harris exercised, largely through the various positions he occupied at the MCC, that he has at times been vilified as a narrow-minded and humourless autocrat. Benny Green deduces from a photograph that Lord Harris had 'half-crazed eyes', and devotes a whole chapter of his *A History of Cricket* (1988) to a lengthy character assassination. Certainly he was imposing and intimidating, in both manner and

*Taunton 1896, the year after Lord Harris's return from India when he was still
appearing occasionally for Kent. Standing: E.B. Shine, H.B. Stewart,
W.M. Bradley, C.J. Burnup; seated: G.J.V. Weigall, W.H. Patterson,
F. Marchant, Lord Harris, J.R. Mason; front: F. Martin, F.H. Huish.*

appearance, but so were a great many Edwardian aristocrats, born and brought up as they
were to become leaders and give orders. The mistake of his detractors has been to allow
themselves to be prejudiced by his apparent haughty authoritarianism and to try and
judge him not by the standards of his own time but those of nearly a century later.

His manner notwithstanding, Lord Harris was arguably the most significant reformer
in cricket's history. Certainly he was leagues ahead of most of his contemporaries in his
views on the treatment of professionals, respect for the Laws and a general determination
that the standards of play should be improved wherever possible, an opinion upheld by
Ric Sissons in *The Players* (1988): 'Lord Harris occupies a mighty place in the history of
cricket and his concern for the welfare of the professionals was exemplary in comparison
to the shoddy treatment dispensed by many county Committees.'

His devotion to cricket was single-minded, as was his belief that certain fundamental
obstacles were holding up the game's natural progress and evolution. This accounts for
the uncompromising stance he took over the two issues of the registration of county
players and bowlers with dubious actions. It was not unknown for his lordship to accost a
player at the start of a match and demand to know how he was qualified to play for the
county in question. And yet there were few contemporary professionals who did not

agree that he was fair – if fierce. Single-minded though he may have been about cricket, it by no means controlled his life. At no other time in the game's history could one contemplate a man captaining his county – and doing so in a fully active manner – and serving in the government, as Lord Harris did between 1885 and 1889 when he was Under-Secretary for India and for War.

Lord Harris was the leading power in cricket in 1895, and equally there was no doubt as to who was the leading player: W.G. Grace. This was despite the fact that the previous few seasons had marked a slowing-down in his run-scoring. During the five seasons of 1890–94 (including a tour to Australia in 1891–92) he could only manage a total of six centuries. For much of the previous twenty years he had scored that many each season. And he was getting on; he would celebrate his 47th birthday in July.

All the same, the Old Man approached the new season with a total of 98 centuries and the tantalizing prospect of making it 100 – more than double what any other batsman had ever made. He wasted no time and in his first major game of the season, for MCC and Ground against Sussex at Lord's he made 103 in the second innings: 99 and one to go. The next match was again at Lord's and no doubt many observers – among them Lord Harris – would have considered it entirely suitable that 100 hundreds should first be reached within the hallowed portals. Playing for the MCC against Yorkshire, Grace was not surprisingly given no quarter by the northern men and could only manage 18 and 25.

However strong his allegiance to the MCC (he usually wore the club's hooped cap perched on his head when batting), Grace was first and foremost a Gloucestershire man and there is little question that he himself would most enjoy reaching the milestone in his home county. And so as he travelled west for Gloucestershire's next match at Bristol he must have hoped that the time had come – added to which the match was against the county's neighbouring rivals Somerset, captained by one of Grace's best cricketing friends, Sammy Woods. It was a friendship based on the two men's similar appetites for life and their extraordinary energy, and punctuated with regular banter. Woods referred to Grace as an 'artful toad' and maintained that 'you couldn't make the Old Man drunk because his nut was too large'. For his part Grace always referred to Woods as 'shock 'ead' and knew that he was a dependable partner for a late-night game of whist accompanied by a few bottles of champagne.

It could hardly have been a more enjoyable prospect, and Grace rose to the occasion. It was bitterly cold, although reports that it snowed – in mid-May! – are probably a fanciful embellishment of the legend, but the weather proved no deterrent. Somerset batted first and appeared to be taking control of the match when their openers, L.C.H. Palairet and G. Fowler, put on 205 for the first wicket. They went on to score 303, Grace taking five for 87. He was bowling when the visitors were all out, but quarter of an hour later reappeared to open the Gloucestershire innings. By the close of play he had made 32. The next day, with the Grace clan out in force among the spectators, he progressed relentlessly until finally, with his score on 98, Sammy Woods pitched up a full-toss which was sent to the leg-side boundary. The ground erupted and Grace's brother, E.M., who had so often batted with W.G. for Gloucestershire during the previous thirty-odd years, was supposed to have said wistfully, 'I would have given a year of my life – almost anything – to have been in with him when he made that hit.'

A BOUNDARY!

PLAY!

ALWAYS FIRST ON THE FIELD.

AT POINT.

CRICKETERS IN THE FIELD.
W. G. GRACE.

W.G., more studied by cartoonists than any other cricketer and usually the same genial but imposing figure.

The 100th hundred was an historic landmark, but in Grace's progress through the season it soon took on the appearance of a brief resting-post. In the short term he showed scant gratitude for Woods's indulgence by going on to make 288. The return to his old style of batting was confirmed more than anything else by the fact that in five and a half hours he had only missed four balls. The size of this score stirred the possibility of another hitherto unapproached record, 1,000 runs before the end of May.

After scoring 52 for the Gentlemen against Cambridge, Grace travelled with Gloucestershire to Gravesend to play Kent. His efforts against Somerset had demonstrated that neither his age nor his bulk had affected his stamina, but his display during this match was even more remarkable. He was on the field for every moment of the three days, batting throughout Gloucestershire's first innings to make 257 before being the last man out and, after a long stint in the field, leading a successful chase for runs in their second by scoring 73 in an hour. The Old Man was not only unstoppable but inexhaustible.

Grace had now scored 829 runs since 9 May and had two matches left before the end of the month. The first was Walter Read's benefit match at The Oval between England and Surrey, but Tom Richardson put paid to the huge crowd's hopes by bowling Grace for 18. So to Lord's for Gloucestershire's game against Middlesex, beginning on 30 May, with Grace needing to score 153. With the nation on tenterhooks, Grace won the toss and batted. After an unusually cautious start he got into his stride once past 50; as he approached his 100 the only danger was that he would run out of partners as the other Gloucestershire men were falling all too regularly, but late in the afternoon a boundary took him from 149 to the magic 153 and 1,000 runs in May. In the end he scored 169 which made a total of 1,019 runs in 22 days since 9 May. Of the select group of seven other men who have since reached 1,000 runs before the end of May, only two – Walter Hammond and Charlie Hallows – have done so within the calendar month.

Having achieved more in the space of a few weeks than most batsmen hoped for throughout a whole season, Grace might have been forgiven for easing the pace. But the only respite he took advantage of was enforced by the weather which intervened regularly in June and July. By the end of the season he had scored five more hundreds, including his first for the Gentlemen against the Players at Lord's for 19 years, and an aggregate 2,346 runs, a total he had only ever exceeded when aged 23 and 28. It was easily more than any other batsman that year and only MacLaren's innings of 424 put him above Grace in the averages.

The year 1895 confirmed Grace's extraordinary genius as a cricketer at the same time as adding to it a new dimension, for no cricketer would ever again put up a remotely comparable performance at anything approaching his age. It also produced a flood of national affection and congratulation: a message from the Prince of Wales, three separate testimonials which together grossed nearly £10,000, and thousands of words in newspapers and journals extolling the greatness of Grace. The Victorians and Edwardians always made the most of opportunities to hero-worship their national figures. But never before had any sportsman been lionized in such a manner, and the accolade afforded to Grace cannot be so dismissed. In simple terms the combination of his background, personality and characteristics, the intriguing blend of simplicity and modesty with zest

BANQUET

HELD ON

MONDAY, JUNE 24TH, 1895, at the VICTORIA ROOMS, CLIFTON,

TO

MR W. G. GRACE

in Celebration of his

ONE HUNDREDTH "CENTURY,"

Completed on GLOUCESTERSHIRE COUNTY GROUND in match

SOMERSETSHIRE v GLOUCESTERSHIRE,

on FRIDAY MAY 17TH 1895.

HIS GRACE THE DUKE OF BEAUFORT, K.G.,

President

Grace's county Gloucestershire celebrated his 100 hundreds with a banquet. The doctor often rode to hounds with the president, the Duke of Beaufort.

*W.G. and Tom Richardson (seated to his right), playing together for the
former's London County side against Wiltshire in 1904. The doctor's side also
included his old crony Billy Murdoch (sitting on the extreme left) and Johnny
Douglas, on the ground in front of Richardson.*

and spontaneity, the fact that he was not tied to any one class and, not least, his never-to-
be-forgotten appearance meant that any sort of Englishman could identify with him.

From 1895 onwards he became a national monument, to whom small boys were taken
up to shake hands, although, as George Lyttelton recalled, never did Grace allow his
elevated status to suppress his natural instincts and basic, almost rustic, sense of humour.

My father knew him well and took my brother and me to shake his hand after a match
at Worcester in 1897. He was very gracious in a sort of Newfoundland doglike way –
more so than to another parent who had also presented his son to him. The first thing
the old man said to the boy, his father standing by, was 'Well, young fellow, I hope yer
a better fielder than your father was; he was the worst I ever did see!' and went off into
a Gargantuan laugh.

Grace's partner when he hit Sammy Woods to the boundary for his 100th hundred was a gangling 18-year-old called Charles Townsend, and other than a member of Grace's own family there could not have been a more suitable person to have been in with him. While Grace was Gloucestershire's great veteran, Townsend was the county's youthful prodigy. His father, Frank, was a close friend of W.G.'s, having been a leading light of the Gloucestershire XI during the Grace-family-dominated years of success in the 1870s. It would be hard to imagine anyone with a more different physique from Grace's expansive frame; indeed, together they looked like a couple of caricatures. C.B. Fry remembered that when Townsend once travelled to Yorkshire for a match some disrespectful tyke shouted from the crowd, 'yon lad's 'asn't enough fat on 'im to grease a gimlet', and Townsend's Gloucestershire compatriot G.L. Jessop wrote in his memoirs that, 'one felt as he lumbered up to the crease on his way to deliver the ball, that, as a matter of expediency, it were well to provide the umpire with baskets to pick up the pieces in the event of Charles breaking in two.'

Charles Townsend exemplified the late-Victorian and Edwardian phenomenon of the brilliant schoolboy cricketer. Having displayed a rare degree of skill at a precociously early age, he first played for Gloucestershire when still at school, aged 16, and his first-class career was all but over before he was 25. He was still only 22 in 1899 when he won a place in two Tests against Australia. During the early years he was principally a bowler – slow right-arm-over – bowling off-breaks and leg-breaks, often with a prodigious amount of spin. His batting came to the fore around 1898, and when he was chosen for England in 1899 he was the best left-hander in the country.

C.L. Townsend, tall and deceptively frail-looking, who
exemplified the schoolboy cricketing prodigy.

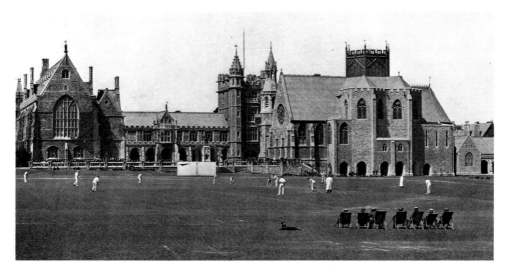

Clifton's immortal Close, during the Edwardian period when spectating at major matches was compulsory for the rest of the school.

Townsend was a product of Clifton, perhaps the most representative cricketing school of the period, scene of Newbolt's 'breathless hush' and second only to Eton in the number of boys it sent on to play county cricket as amateurs during the period: 13, including two county captains. And in 1899 schoolboy history was made when 13-year-old Arthur Collins batted for over six hours to score 628 in a junior house match. It remains the highest individual score on record. Collins became a lieutenant in the Royal Engineers and survived only the first three months of the war.

Townsend first made an impact beyond Clifton's immortal Close in 1893 when he was picked for Gloucestershire. He took 5 for 70 against the Australians and then, in the Cheltenham Festival against Somerset, established a record which has yet to be equalled: a hat-trick of three stumpings. But as his frail appearance suggested, he was not yet robust enough for the rigours of first-class cricket and his proper introduction did not come until late in 1895. His appearance in W.G.'s match against Somerset in May – when he scored 95 – was to be his only one until the end of July. From then until the end of the season he took 122 wickets in 11 matches, including 94 in August, an unequalled total for one month. In a description of Townsend's action H.S. Altham gives an insight into his effectiveness:

> Tall, and bowling with a high action, he was very difficult to 'get at': on a wicket that gave him any help he spun the ball viciously and could make it lift, whilst on a true pitch one of his deadliest weapons was the patent leg-break that in fact went straight on. At his best he could be lethal, the more so because at the time leg-break bowling was an almost forgotten art.

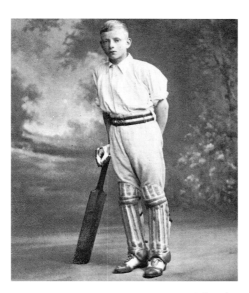

*Arthur Collins, who made history at Clifton but
was killed in action after only three months of the war.*

Admittedly he was assisted by damp wickets but in no way did this detract from his performance, and his haul of wickets in successive matches reads like the usually well-spread highlights of most bowlers' careers. Nottinghamshire were his main victims: 16 wickets at Trent Bridge and 13 in the return fixture at Cheltenham. In addition he took 15 Yorkshire wickets at Cheltenham and 12 on three occasions: against Sussex at Bristol, Surrey at Clifton and Somerset at Taunton. He ended the season having bowled 746 overs and taken 131 wickets at just less than 14 runs apiece. He was only pipped from topping the national averages by Captain W.C. Hedley (later Colonel Sir Walter Hedley), a fast-medium amateur with one of the most questionable actions of the time which was eventually denounced at the 1900 county captains' meeting by eleven votes to one.

There could have been no greater contrast between this pale and reticent boy and Tom Richardson, the man relegated in the national averages for 1895 by Townsend's August performance. Admittedly, at 25 Richardson was also young, but from the day that he first appeared for Surrey in 1892 there were few cricketers who could rival his magnificent physique and strength. Topped by a dense mane of jet-black hair and adorned with a ferocious, full black moustache he was an unforgettable sight, and it is not surprising that there were suspicions that he had gypsy blood and that C.B. Fry described him as a 'cheerful brown-faced Italian-looking brigand'.

In fact any hint of hostility was an illusion for Richardson was one of the most genial, modest and friendly cricketers of this or any period. His standard remark to young amateurs who passed him on their way back to the pavilion after he had shattered their wicket was, 'Best one I've bowled all season, sir.' All the same, very few people have questioned his claim to have been the greatest fast bowler of all time. Cardus reserved

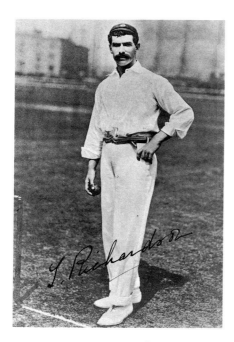

*Tom Richardson, for C.B. Fry 'a cheerful brigand' and the greatest fast bowler
of the Edwardian period, and as portrayed in the hugely popular halfpenny
weekly,* Ally Sloper's Half Holiday.

some of his most effusive and romantic language for Richardson, 'the cricketer whose
heart was so big that even his large body hardly contained its heroic energy'; a less
elaborate judgement was given by H.S. Altham:

> There have been faster bowlers, though they could be counted on the fingers of one
> hand; there have been deadlier bowlers, though on a hard wicket very, very few; but
> for sustained excellence, day in day out, Richardson need fear comparison with none
> of his own order; physically and spiritually he was cast in the mould of Alfred Mynn.

The summer of 1895 was the peak in a run of successive seasons when Richardson
bowled thousands of overs with a consistency that one can only marvel at. In the one
season he took 290 wickets at an average of just over 14 and bowled nearly 1,700 overs.
That total of 290 has only ever been exceeded twice: by Tich Freeman who took 304 and
298 in 1928 and 1933. And Freeman bowled around 2,000 overs in each season, but the
comparison is laughable. Freeman jogged up to the wicket for four or five yards and
wheeled his arm over. Richardson cantered – at times thundered – in from well over
three or four times that distance, and delivered the ball with a high leap, stretching
action and scythe-like follow-through that as often as not produced his usually unplayable
break-back ball.

During the four seasons from 1894 to 1897 (excluding the tour to Australia in 1894–95 when he was the decisive bowler) Richardson took 1,005 wickets at an average of 14 runs. No fast bowler has ever approached such an achievement and neither has any bowler – fast or slow – approached the short space of time it took him to pass the career milestones of 1,000 and 2,000 wickets. Among the select band of 32 English bowlers who have ever taken 2,000 wickets, Richardson played for 13 seasons and only two others have reached the total in fewer than 20. But Richardson did not play for his figures. He bowled to take wickets, and the mathematics of what he achieved would have been of minor importance to him. One thing is certain: he would never have resented the fact that at the end of the 1895 season a young schoolboy amateur had pipped him in the averages by less than half a point.

Richardson's bowling during that season was the major factor in Surrey retaining the championship for the second year in succession. Considering that The Oval was a batsman's paradise, the contribution of three fast bowlers, George Lohmann, William Lockwood and Richardson, to Surrey's unrivalled ascendancy during the late 1880s and early 1890s is the more impressive. Each one had his own period of supremacy: first Lohmann, followed by Lockwood and then Richardson. Popular imagination has Lockwood and Richardson bowling in tandem throughout the 1890s, but during Richardson's year of triumph in 1895 and the two subsequent seasons Lockwood's contribution was minimal because he subsided into alcoholism. He did not recover until 1898 and in that year the two bowled out Yorkshire in a day at The Oval and George Hirst said afterwards that it was the best bowling he ever had to face: 'no rest at either end'.

It was inevitable that such constant exertion as Richardson underwent would take its toll, and after he returned from his second tour of Australia in 1897–98 he was never quite the tower of strength he had been before. No doubt his liking for beer – one contemporary reckoned that he drank a bottle for every hour of his bowling – contributed to his rapid gain in weight, and at the end of the 1904 season he retired from the Surrey side. He became a publican, first in Bath and subsequently in his native Surrey, but was dogged by ill-health until, in 1912 when he was in the South of France, convalescing, he died aged 41. At the time it was suspected that he committed suicide, but it has been established that the cause was either cerebral congestion or a heart attack. It was a poignantly early death for a man who, perhaps more than any other, had typified the raw, earthy vigour of the period. With or without his stupendous records he would always have been remembered by those who watched him bowling as one of the most stimulating sights they had experienced. In his correspondence with Rupert Hart-Davis, George Lyttelton replies to the argument that E.A. MacDonald was the most beautiful bowler to watch by simply saying, 'you are talking to one who saw Tom Richardson'.

Tom Richardson typified one kind of Edwardian cricketer who, brimming with an apparent tirelessness, perfected his art through hours of work. In a very different mould was A.C. MacLaren, the one cricketer who evoked from Cardus even greater hyperbole than he used in his descriptions of Richardson. As Richardson was toiling his way through the 1895 summer, bowling out county sides in match after match, MacLaren stepped out at Taunton one July morning and embarked on an innings which, as well as staying

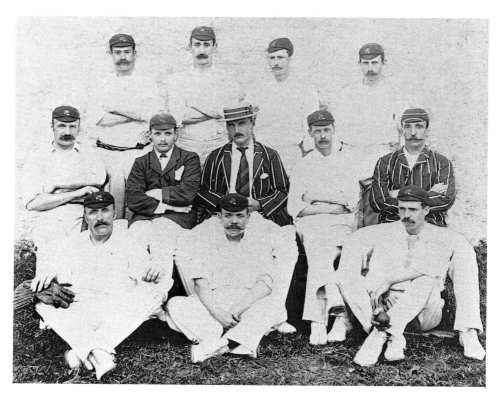

Archie MacLaren and his Lancashire side at Taunton for the historic match
against Somerset.

in the record books ever since, was of huge significance at the time. While W.G. Grace was carrying all before him here was a young man just about half his age who had the audacity to pass the Old Man's record of 344 set up nearly twenty years before, and at the same time signalling that there was a new generation of batsmen about to unleash a flood of run-scoring over the next decade or so.

The circumstances of MacLaren's innings are typical of his whole career. In 1894 he had established himself as the captain of Lancashire at the age of 22. During the winter he toured Australia with A.E. Stoddart and, especially during the latter matches, batted with outstanding success. Early in the 1895 season he failed in a couple of matches and then, precariously short of money as was so often the case, took a job teaching at a prep school in Harrow, close to his old Alma Mater. Considering that he was still the county captain, this caused understandable feeling among the ranks of Lancashire supporters — and elsewhere, as hinted at by Sammy Woods, the captain of Somerset, when he heard that MacLaren would be returning to captain Lancashire for the game at Taunton: 'A.C. MacLaren kindly consented to play against us.'

SOMERSET COUNTY CRICKET GROUND,

TAUNTON, JULY 15th, 16th & 17th, 1895.

SOMERSET v. LANCASHIRE.

LANCASHIRE. First Innings.		Second Innings.	
1 A. C. MacLaren c Fowler b Gamlin	424*		
2 Ward c R. Palairet b Tyler	64		
3 Paul c Gamlin b L. Palairet	177		
4 Sugg c Wickham b Woods	41		
5 Tinsley c Gamlin b Woods	0		
6 Baker st Wickham b L. Palairet	23		
7 Briggs not out	9		
8 C. H. Benton c and b Fowler	43		
9 Smith c Trask b L. Palairet	0		
10 Hallam c Fowler b L. Palairet	6		
11 Mold c R. Palairet b Gamlin	0		
B 9, l-b 4, w 1	14		
Total	801†	Total	

1-141 2-504 3-530 4-637 5-732 6-738 7-792 8-792 9-798 10-801
1- 2- 3- 4- 5- 6- 7- 8- 9- 10-

SOMERSET. First Innings.		Second Innings.	
1 L. C. H. Palairet b Briggs	30	b Mold	4
2 G. Fowler c Sub. b Hallam	39	c MacLaren b Mold	46
3 R. C. N. Palairet c Hallam b Mold	2	st Smith b Briggs	7
4 H. T. Stanley c Smith b Briggs	8	c Smith b Mold	12
5 R. B. Porch run out	18	c MacLaren b Mold	1
6 S. M. J. Woods c Smith b Mold	11	b Briggs	55
7 Dr. J. E. Trask c Ward b Mold	11	c and b Mold	26
8 Tyler not out	15	b Briggs	41
9 E. W. Bartlett b Briggs	4	c Mold b Briggs	6
10 Rev. A. P. Wickham b Mold	3	not out	0
11 Gamlin st Smith b Briggs	0	hit wkt. b Briggs	0
L-b 2	2	B 4, l-b 4	8
Total	143	Total	206

1-71 2-73 3-73 4-94 5-107 6-121 7-122 8-132 9-137 10-143
1-5 2-61 3-61 4-83 5-150 6-151 7-187 8-206 9-206 10-206

Umpires—J. Wickens & F. N. Lowe.   Scorers—T. H. Knight & S. Lunt.

* RECORD for highest Individual Score in First-Class Cricket.

† RECORD for highest Innings in County Cricket.

The scorecard.

Never being one to take criticism lightly, it is certain that Archie was determined to silence any rumbling. He did so in the most emphatic manner possible. Winning the toss, he opened the batting and by the close of play had made 289. Lancashire's score was 555 for three and MacLaren and A.G. Paul had put on 363 for the second wicket. Overnight W.G. Grace was sporting enough to send a telegram: 'Hearty congratulations on Archie's grand performance hope he will break the record.' Shortly after noon the following day he did so and before lunch had not only passed 400 but also scored a hundred in the morning session. The end came during the afternoon when, understandably tired, MacLaren was caught in the deep for 424. Prevented by the law from declaring, Lancashire went on to score 801, at the time another record.

MacLaren's runs were scored in a manner which he made all his own and which inspired Cardus's well-worn description 'the Noblest Roman'. It was the blend of arrogance and power, and his unfailing ability to produce a stroke to attack any kind of delivery, which left an indelible impression on all who watched him, as demonstrated years later by one of the Somerset fielders:

> MacLaren's stance at the wicket as the ball was delivered was majestic. All he did was done in the grand style. The end of his bat was pointing straight at the sky above his head and his hands were about level with his right shoulder. I do not suppose that absolutely every stroke started like that but that was the main impression . . . Let the bowler pitch the ball where he liked there would be an unhurried stroke with a full swing to counter it.

Sammy Woods, who bore the brunt of the Somerset bowling, had far less romantic memories of the occasion: 'I thought the day would never end. I must have run miles.'

Glorious batsman though he was, MacLaren illustrated the shortcomings of the strict divisions which ruled cricket, for he could never really afford to play as an amateur. He was born into a large family of boys whom the father was determined to send to Harrow, but in the event funds only stretched to the eldest three – including Archie – being sent there. It was at Harrow that Archie acquired his formidable batting technique and first demonstrated that he was something out of the ordinary; aged 15 he scored 55 and 67 in his first Eton v. Harrow match at Lord's. It was also where he probably acquired his tendency to disguise with bravado the feelings of inferiority prompted by his aristocratic and well-off schoolfellows and to give himself airs, so that even Cardus remarked, 'where he got his flavours of blue blood from I never could tell or find out'. George Lyttelton's later memories of Archie are distinctly caustic. 'It is disillusioning to one of my youthful loyalties to realise that the Majestic MacLaren, with his "superb crease-side manner", was an extremely stupid, prejudiced and pig-headed man.'

Whatever MacLaren's personal shortcomings, they paled into insignificance whenever he took to the cricket field, except, as we shall see, on one or two celebrated occasions when they clouded his judgements as a captain. But in 1895 he scaled the heights along with Grace, Townsend and Richardson, both to make it a year of landmarks and – one can say with hindsight – to launch a new era of cricket.

4

AMATEURS AND PROFESSIONALS: PASTIME OR JOB?

In simplified terms English cricket between 1895 and 1914 can be seen as a cake, of which the professionals contributed the essential mixture and the amateurs the icing. Without the professionals there would have been no organized first-class cricket at all, no county competition. Without the amateurs it would have existed, but it would have been a good deal duller. The two complemented each other to such an extent because at no other time in the game's history have their different – and at times overlapping – contributions been so evenly balanced. It has often been maintained that the distinction between amateurs and professionals was imposed to conform with the rigid social structure of the time. While it is true that the division reflected the general state of the nation, this was not the cause of the situation which was prompted by changes in cricket rather than in society – although, of course, the two cannot always be separated.

There were two fundamental reasons for the division. First, with the expansion of the first-class game and the number of players involved, the advent of a proper county competition and the general elevation of cricket's status, it was necessary to formalize the distinction between those who played cricket as a pastime, and therefore could expect neither financial nor employment commitments from their county committees, and those for whom cricket was a job, a livelihood. This second category, the professionals, was the most important, for there was the greatest need to improve their conditions generally and to establish some degree of uniformity of terms offered by the counties. The second reason was the abundance of amateurs with both the time and the talent to play county cricket.

The usual conception of an Edwardian county side is that it consisted of a backbone of professionals adorned with one or two amateurs. Generally speaking this was the case, although some counties – notably Kent and Middlesex who maintained a strong amateur tradition, and some of the lesser counties recently elevated to first-class status who lacked the resources to pay five or six full-time professionals, such as Somerset and Leicestershire – usually had more amateurs. What it disguises, however, is the quantity of amateurs compared to professionals who played during the period. Between 1895 and 1914 there were 603 county cricketers, of whom 325 were professionals and 278 amateurs. The totals are surprisingly even – only a 7 per cent difference.

W.G. on his 50th birthday captaining the Gentlemen of 1898 against the
Players. Standing: C.J. Kortright, J.R. Mason, A.C. MacLaren,
J.A. Dixon, West (umpire); seated: S.M.J. Woods, A.E. Stoddart, W.G. Grace,
C.L. Townsend, F.S. Jackson; front: Capt. Wynyard, G. MacGregor.

The high number of amateurs ensured that their influence and the distinctive flavour they gave to the game were maintained constantly throughout the period, which would not have been otherwise possible. The most important contrast between them and professionals was the length of time they played for. The figures here are tellingly different. While amateurs played an average of just over three and a half seasons, professionals averaged six and a half. Of the 101 players who remained in a county side for ten seasons or more, 78 – or 77 per cent – were professionals. At the other end of the scale, 49 per cent of amateurs played for one or two seasons only, as opposed to 29 per cent of professionals.

The reason for the short careers of the majority of amateurs was simple. Most of them played first-class cricket as an enjoyable interlude while they were young men between leaving school and taking up their chosen occupation. With very few exceptions, these being a handful of wealthy (and usually aristocratic) grandees, such as Lord Dalmeny who became the sixth Earl of Rosebery, Charles de Trafford (whose father sold the Old Trafford ground to Lancashire in 1894 for £24,000) and his brother-in-law Sir Timothy O'Brien, third Baronet, the great majority of amateurs took up jobs which only rarely allowed them time for first-class cricket.

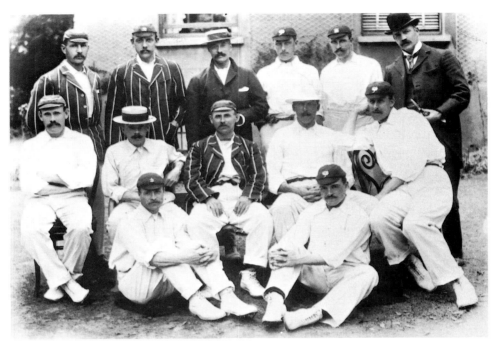

The Players' team that opposed Grace on his 50th birthday and achieved a closely-fought victory. Standing: W.H. Lockwood, J.T. Hearne, W. Brockwell, W. Rhodes, A.A. Lilley, West (umpire); seated: W. Storer, R. Abel, A. Shrewsbury, J. Gunn, J. Tunnicliffe; front: A. Hearne, S. Haigh.

The careers of 35 per cent of amateurs began with a blue at Oxford or Cambridge. It was a small minority who either committed themselves to cricket to the extent of delaying – and thereby possibly endangering – their future occupation, or were good enough to be able to command a place in a county side on an occasional basis. Certainly there were notorious cases of professionals being summarily removed for a match or two to make way for an amateur who did not qualify on merit, especially during festivals towards the end of the season, such as Canterbury Week when the number of amateurs in the Kent side was always higher than usual. This was also the time of year when schoolmasters were available or other amateurs could play in a few games during their own holiday. But instances of social superiority prevailing over ability were the exception rather than the rule; it would have been unthinkable for Lord Hawke to have ordered one of his Yorkshire regulars to make way for a part-time amateur.

The most serious failing of the amateur/professional system concerned those players who could not afford financially to play as amateurs and yet could not afford socially to play as professionals – the disguised professional. As Ric Sissons writes, 'The disguised professional was created by social and class pressures on middle-class cricketers who lacked the independent financial means to play as true amateurs and who could not accept

Their lordships' toss: Lord Dalmeny — captain of Surrey,
later Earl of Rosebery — with Lord Hawke at The Oval.

the stigma of being a professional.' In such cases the ethos of amateurism held so dear by the Edwardians broke down and became a sham. W.G. Grace himself is sometimes cited as the prime offender, but his case is not representative in that his reputation was vastly greater than any other cricketer's. If the *Daily Telegraph*'s testimonial fund raised almost £9,000 in 1895 to celebrate his 100th hundred it was not a reflection on W.G.'s amateur status but his popularity.

Certainly, however, there were cases when amateurs were unquestionably paid on a regular 'salaried' basis, Archie MacLaren, and Walter Read of Surrey being two. Both occupied the loosely defined position of assistant secretary for their county clubs which brought them a salary at the same time as they appeared full time as players. Both were paid more money by their counties than any of the respective professionals — and Surrey and Lancashire were two of the most prosperous, highest-paying counties.

Such arrangements were not designed to create good relations with the professionals. In many ways, however, considering the number of amateurs who played, the vague terms of most of their arrangements over 'expenses' and the fact that a great many of them were not well off, the cases could have been much more widespread. That they were not was more due to the strength of the professionals in most counties and the fact that the great majority of amateurs had relatively short careers, than to scrupulous county committees.

It is difficult to generalize about relations between amateurs and professionals, but it was far more often a case of friendship — albeit fairly distant and formal — based on mutual respect for each other's ability than the sort of situation described by the Australian captain Joe Darling, writing in his memoirs about the 1902 tour: 'I have heard some

English captains speak to their professionals like dogs.' On a number of occasions such behaviour got its just deserts: Sir Timothy O'Brien was renowned for his somewhat overbearing manner, but after one contretemps Surrey refused to play Middlesex if O'Brien was in the side and Middlesex had to agree.

Given that amateurs were often young and inexperienced, they regarded established professionals, in particular the county's senior pro, with considerable respect and admiration. Most of them would have been coached by a professional at their schools – as George Hirst and Wilfred Rhodes were to become at Eton and Harrow respectively, the former a great success the latter not so – and learnt to appreciate what could be taught to them by cricketers who had succeeded not by talent alone but by unstinting hard work and reliability. Young men who thought otherwise did not last very long in county sides.

Amateur captains may have been compulsory but a great many of them regularly consulted senior professionals over strategy both on and off the field: bowling changes, field-placing, batting order, etc.; although it is nothing more than a good story that any of them ever abdicated the job to the supposed extent of Lord Hawke's successor as captain of Yorkshire, who was approached in the field by one of his pros and told, 'Come in, sir, Wilfred's [Rhodes] declared.'

Bad relations between amateur and professional players were rare and usually arose in instances of personal differences between two strong characters. C.B. Fry's conceited manner did not always endear him to professionals and he enjoyed a series of skirmishes with Nottinghamshire's Tom Wass who once rounded on Fry (who had addressed him as

'Topsy' Wass, Notts opening bowler, who worked as a
miner every winter and had scant respect for social niceties.

'Wass') with the words, 'It's Mister Wass to buggers such as thee.' 'Topsy' Wass, who was born and died in the Nottinghamshire coal-mining village of Sutton-in-Ashfield and worked down the mine each winter during his 25-year career with Nottinghamshire, was certainly one of the richest characters among the professionals. A fast-medium bowler with a devastating fast leg-break, during the early 1900s he was probably good enough to have played for England; Ashley-Cooper considered that, 'on his day, he was the most deadly bowler in England', but it was rumoured that he was never picked because his table manners were so dreadful.

During a county game, of course, that would not have mattered because amateurs and professionals had lunch separately. While the amateurs ate in the pavilion – the cost of their lunch included in their expenses – the professionals fended for themselves. Especially for the bowlers, this usually meant a visit to the beer tent for a pint or two and, as Wilfred Rhodes remembered, it was often difficult to limit consumption when well-meaning supporters were not to be dissuaded from showing their appreciation with a free drink. It was only after the turn of the century that amateurs and professionals began to eat in the same room – and even then at separate tables, and the food was usually different. The situation did not arise at tea-time because the interval was not formalized before 1914. Batsmen could request a drink, although few were as confident as Nottinghamshire's George Gunn who would order a cup of tea to be brought out at 4.15 as he went out to bat during the early afternoon.

Although by the standards of the day the segregation at lunch was inevitable, it was one of a number of petty divisions imposed to formalize the relationship between amateur and professional which often caused far greater offence to the professionals than any personal differences they may have had with amateurs. There was a fine line between distinctions that were accepted as a normal part of life, and those that were clearly imposed for no good reason other than social emphasis.

Players used separate dressing rooms – again, inevitable by the standards of the day, but it understandably riled many pros to know that upstairs perhaps two or three amateurs shared a room twice the size of one which accommodated ten or more professionals, that the amateurs had a prime view of the ground while they were probably in the basement with no view at all and that the amateurs had a bath each while they had a couple of tin tubs to pull underneath taps. It was exactly as life was led outside the cricket world; the problem was that the close proximity emphasized the gap to an – at times – exasperating degree.

From their separate dressing rooms they used separate gates onto the ground, the amateurs usually coming down the central steps of the pavilion, the professionals emerging from a more modest side-gate. Other than for opening batsmen, who were forced to rendezvous halfway to the wicket in an unnecessarily formal and almost comic fashion, this did not always bother the professionals. Given the strong loyalties which bound them together in a manner which never occurred with amateurs, most would have agreed with Alec Bedser when he said about his early years at The Oval that he 'would far rather walk out of the gate that Jack Hobbs had used than any other gate in the world'. It was a measure of Lord Hawke's respect for his pros that Yorkshire was the first county to abolish separate gates.

Saturnine Sydney Barnes, the bowling genius who saw no
reason to kowtow to either amateurs or the authorities.

The standard travel arrangements to away matches, whereby amateurs travelled first-class and the professionals went third together, were as it would have normally been in everyday life. But again, it was not always seen to be exactly fair that an amateur travelled first-class regardless of whether he could personally afford to or not, because his expenses were paid by the county, while the professionals paid for their tickets out of their wages.

As Tom Wass made clear to Fry, forms of address could often be a bone of contention. So respected and senior a player as Frank Woolley would never have addressed Lord Harris other than as 'your lordship' until his dying day – nor would he have expected his lordship to call him anything other than 'Woolley' or possibly 'Frank'. But at times the convention appeared somewhat forced when a 40-year-old senior pro, probably one of the most famous cricketers in England, was compelled to address a 17-year-old schoolboy as 'sir' or 'Mr Fotherington-Snooks'. Nonetheless, amateurs were always addressed in this way, and the professionals by their surnames only, or occasionally by their Christian names or nicknames. The distinction was emphasized on scorecards and in match reports in the papers.

Quite a few professionals objected to both the formalities of their position and the terms of their employment. Virtually all of them put up with it, with one famous exception: Sydney Francis Barnes. Barnes was abrasive and outspoken in his conversation, and his appearance and bowling were in the same vein. He stood well over six foot, usually looked at batsmen with a deep frown if not a scowl, and had only one intention: to send them back to the pavilion as quickly as possible, which he was always confident of doing. Blending with this formidable, uncompromising attitude was unrivalled technical brilliance as a bowler. The combination for batsmen was an unnerving experience.

As well as standing head and shoulders above most of his contemporaries, where Barnes was unusual among professionals was in his fierce independence which led him to turn his back on the county game and spend most of his career playing league cricket. He was not going to be patronized by a county secretary who had probably only ever played in a junior house match at school, and he usually left people in no doubt of his feelings. Amongst the game's authorities he was regarded with considerable suspicion as a rebel, which partly accounted for his limited Test appearances despite his superlative performances.

After playing four games for Warwickshire during the 1890s Barnes got fed up and left. He moved to Lancashire but did not appear regularly until Lancashire's captain, Archie MacLaren, took up his cause. MacLaren was in no doubt as to Barnes's qualities as a bowler, but he was often sorely tested by his manner. When he was leading the 1901–02 side in Australia – of which Barnes was a member at MacLaren's instigation – the team were caught on board ship in very rough seas which prompted MacLaren to say with feeling, 'Well, at least if we go down we'll take that bugger Barnes with us.'

The MacLaren–Barnes situation is pertinent in that, despite their personal differences, these did not interfere with the high regard that they had for each other as cricketers. MacLaren picked Barnes for his 1901–02 tour on the strength of having seen him bowl in one county game – for Lancashire against Leicestershire – when Barnes took six for 70, and after batting against him in a net at Old Trafford. When Barnes apologized for hitting MacLaren he got the reply, 'Don't be sorry, Barnes, you're coming to Australia with me.' It was one of MacLaren's inspired gambles and only foundered when Barnes broke down during the Third Test. For Barnes's part, a strong reason for him staying with Lancashire for two full seasons in 1902 and 1903 was his respect for MacLaren as a captain. When he left in 1904 after failing to secure the financial security he felt that he deserved from the Lancashire secretary, MacLaren was furious with the county committee.

Barnes's case was typical in that if a professional had grievances or objections they were usually against his county committee who decided the terms of players' employment. At the beginning of the period a good many county committees regarded their professional cricketers as labourers whom they could hire and fire as they wished and who were expected to accept whatever terms were offered without complaint. By 1914 the situation was very different. County committees had universally accepted – sometimes without much grace – certain basic principles upon which the employment of their professionals was founded. The principles remained the basis of professionals' terms of work until the distinction between them and amateurs disappeared. Financially the amounts often differed from one county to another, but this was a result of the differences in counties' comparative wealth – or lack of it – and because of the complicated system by which the players' fees were made up.

In some ways the steps which led to improvements in the terms offered to professionals were brought about by competition between the counties akin to 'keeping

Lord Harris, a formidable presence and the most powerful
figure in Edwardian cricket.

up with the Joneses'. The better-off counties took the lead so as to guarantee that they would retain the services of their best players. If the poorer counties did not follow suit they risked having their 'stars' poached. But equally as important as such self-interest was the influence of two of cricket's most prominent figures, Lord Harris and Lord Hawke.

Lord Harris was firm and outspoken in his opinion that professionals were fundamental to English cricket and that they had certain important rights, as he made clear on two separate occasions. 'Professional cricketers are absolutely essential if cricket is to be maintained at its present high standard of excellence . . .' he said and, arguing against arbitrary controls over a player's right to move from one county to another, he was adamant in his opposition to, 'anything that had any suspicion of interfering with a working man from selling that which was his property – his labour'.

He was determined to mould what Ric Sissons described as 'the Respectable Professional', a figure who fitted in with his liberal Toryism, who was content if not prosperous and whose employment offered him not only an opportunity to display his talents but also some sort of security. To some extent he succeeded in that in 1914 the leading professionals of the day – Jack Hobbs, Frank Woolley and the Hearnes, for instance – were very different men from some of the rough diamonds of the 1880s and 90s. One thing about Lord Harris could never be doubted: throughout his life his determination and ability to champion the cause of cricketers was formidable. Only a few years before his death his influence was decisive in a legal test case as to the tax liability of a benefit, which was decided in favour of the cricketer. If otherwise, the effect on benefits would have been enormous.

*A Kent group of 1899, containing — as well as the recognizable amateurs — a
good selection of the early products of the Tonbridge Nursery, not least the
youthful Charlie Blythe seated in the centre at the front.*

In Lord Harris's home county of Kent there was a strong tradition of amateur cricket,
but the importance which he attached to having a nucleus of top-class professionals was
demonstrated by the establishment of the Tonbridge Nursery in 1897. Here young
hopefuls were coached from school age until they took up their places in the county side.
In *Barclays World of Cricket* R.L. Arrowsmith described it as an 'astonishing institution'
and pointed to its success by listing the players it had produced before 1914:

Blythe, Humphreys, Fielder, Seymour, Fairservice, Hardinge, Hubble, Woolley,
Preston, Jennings, Collins and Freeman, all of whom had got, or were destined to get,
caps. Besides these it had produced Murrell for Middlesex, Vincett for Sussex,
Badcock for Hampshire and Haywood and Claude Woolley for Northants, while
Hickmott later played for Lancashire.

The rewards were reaped within a few years when Kent won the championship in 1906 —
and did so again three more times before 1914 — for, as Arrowsmith again says, 'no longer
did everything depend on whether certain amateurs were available'.

In Lord Hawke's Yorkshire the situation was different, in that, to all intents and
purposes, the professionals *were* the Yorkshire side. During their peak of success, when

the county retained the championship for three seasons from 1900 to 1902 and lost only two out of sixty matches, other than Lord Hawke himself only three amateurs broke into the magic circle and all of them on an occasional basis. F.S. Jackson could have won a place in any county side even if he only played one match a year; Frank Mitchell was a good enough batsman to top the county's averages in 1901, and Ernest Smith, a schoolmaster and fast bowler, brought welcome freshness to the bowling attack towards the end of the season. Otherwise it was, as Jim Kilburn commented in *Barclays World of Cricket* with characteristic understatement, 'a firmly established side. Lord Hawke himself rarely missed a match. Brown and Tunnicliffe opened the innings, with David Denton and T.L. Taylor following. Wainwright and Hirst were the all-rounders, Haigh and Rhodes the bowlers and David Hunter was wicket-keeper.'

Lord Hawke's motives for improving the players' lot involved a mixture of philanthropy and his ambitions for the county. Certainly he was paternalistic to a degree which has sometimes been sneered at and condemned, but paternalism was a strong characteristic of the age, whether overseas in India or at home in one of the model towns

Professionals personified: the immortal Yorkshire trilogy of Schofield Haigh,
George Hirst (standing) and Wilfred Rhodes, photographed in 1905.

set up by factory owners for their workers, such as Lord Leverhulme's Port Sunlight and the Cadbury family's Bournville. Hawke may have been fanatical about cricket, and Yorkshire cricket in particular, but he was no roaring aristo. The son of a parson, he succeeded unexpectedly to his title after the premature death of his elder brother and, when not involved in cricket – which admittedly took up most of his time either in England or leading winter tours overseas: to North America, Canada, the West Indies, the Argentine, Australia and New Zealand, South Africa and India – he led the life of a country squire at his home, Wighill Park near Tadcaster, conveniently close to Headingley.

Osbert Sitwell, who used to attend the Scarborough Festival as a small boy, on account of his grandfather the first Earl of Londesborough having founded the occasion, was neither then nor later remotely enthusiastic about cricket, but he left an endearing sketch of Lord Hawke in his autobiography, *Left Hand Right Hand!*

> Unappreciative of the game though I was, I derived much pleasure from the company of Lord Hawke, for many years captain of the team. A man of great charm and character, I often as a child reflected how apt was his name, indeed, his features, his shrewd sharp eyes and dark brows and sunburnt face, made him, by some process of name-magic, resemble a hawk; but further than that, no likeness can be traced, for he was very tall and broad, with a slightly shambling gait, and the whole atmosphere round him, and for which he was responsible, was genial and human. Year after year he returned to Scarborough with his team, and when it was not actively engaged he would watch the other matches, and in the intervals of play wander round the ground, seeking out his innumerable young friends and admirers – among whom, in spite of my lack of interest in cricket, I was proud to count myself – and distribute to them peppermint humbugs of an especially vast size out of an enormous paper bag.

For Lord Hawke his professionals were 'my boys', and in many ways he treated them as a schoolmaster of the time would have done his pupils. Discipline was strict: in the early days to get rid of the unruliness which he took on with the captaincy, most notoriously in the well-chronicled, often exaggerated story of his dismissal of Bobby Peel for being drunk, and extended off the field of play. If one of the professionals intended to get married, Lord Hawke expected to meet and approve the prospective bride before the event took place. Most likely she would be taken to Wighill where, every year, he held a party to distribute the money he had allocated to the players as a result of the 'marks' – each worth five shillings – they had gained throughout the season.

Hawke's system of marks replaced the old-established practice of talent money which, if an incentive, had definite limitations. For instance £1 was usually paid for a fifty, but nothing for a more difficult forty-five. In 1898 when Tom Hayward scored 315 not out at The Oval he received £5 talent money from the county secretary which prompted Hayward to remark caustically, 'Well, it's no use me getting three hundred again.' He never did. Hawke awarded marks for good batting and bowling, often regardless of the score or figures achieved, for fielding and catching and probably, it would not be sheer speculation to add, for appearance and behaviour.

Members of the Yorkshire side playing croquet at Wighill Park in 1907,
watched by Lord Hawke (right) and one of his pros, David Denton.

The most significant introduction Lord Hawke made to the finances of his professionals was winter pay. This was the period which witnessed the foundation of professional cricket as a career, and it was the time when winter employment was first accepted as a problem, as it continued to be. In the early days counties accepted no responsibility for their professionals either during the winter or after their retirement. By the mid-1890s some of the leading counties – Surrey, Yorkshire and Lancashire – had begun to give winter pay. In Yorkshire the regulars got £2 per week.

Other counties were often unwilling and at times grudging in following suit, sometimes because they could not afford to, but more usually because leading figures in their clubs held strong views which were most revealing of social attitudes at the time. In 1905 Sir Spencer Ponsonby-Fane, a leading light in Somerset and the highly influential Treasurer of the MCC throughout the period, said that it was 'paying a man to idle away eight months out of twelve', and even just before the war Plum Warner, supposedly as ardent a supporter of cricket and cricketers as they could have hoped to find, was demanding a system which would 'keep the wolf from the door but not be so much that he need not look for employment . . . it was bad from a national point of view that these people should do practically nothing in the winter'. At best such attitudes reflected the Victorian ideals of self-help and paternalism, taken to unrealistic and – even by this time – outdated limits.

Winter pay was a significant step forward for the professional cricketer, even though the amount paid may have been fairly paltry, but a potentially more serious and far more intractable problem was the plight of many cricketers once they had retired from the game. A.W. Pullin – 'Old Ebor' – for many years the main sports writer for the *Yorkshire*

*The Gentlemen of 1901, with only two, MacGregor and Mason, from the
1898 side which opened the chapter. Standing: W.M. Bradley, A.O. Jones,
R.E. Foster, J.R. Mason; seated: D.L.A. Jephson, K.S. Ranjitsinhji,
G. MacGregor, C.M. Wells, C.B. Fry; front: G.L. Jessop, P.F. Warner.*

Post, who sent his match reports from the various Yorkshire grounds by carrier pigeon
back to a loft on the roof of the paper's Leeds office, highlighted the problem in two
melancholy books: *Talks With Old Yorkshire Cricketers*, published in 1898, and *Talks With
Old English Cricketers* (1900). He revealed that a great many players, in their day
outstanding cricketers, had subsided into abject poverty.

About the only way that a professional cricketer could hope to make any serious
provision for life once he had left the game was if he had a successful benefit. But benefits
were very chancy affairs: first, the county committee had to be persuaded that you
deserved one; second, they had to be generous enough to allocate a match with a
reasonable chance of a good gate; third, it could be ruined either by rain or by the match
finishing early. Top matches — such as the Roses match — were never allowed. Only seven
players achieved benefit totals of over £2,000 before 1914 and in the less well-off
counties they could not hope for even half that amount. The desperate importance of a
good benefit and the sad likelihood of failure was most poignantly demonstrated by the
number of players who were prepared to lay out around £150 — for most of them, a year's
pay — to insure against bad weather.

Lord Hawke's response to Pullin's revelations and the problem of benefits was
characteristic. At the same time as persuading the county committee to guarantee that
no benefit would realize less than £1,000 for a Yorkshire player, he insisted that only one-
third of the amount was to be handed over at the time. The rest would be retained and

The opposing Players of 1901 who gained an easy victory at Lord's. Standing:
G. Hirst, R. Carpenter, A.E. Trott, L.C. Braund, West (umpire); seated:
W. Storer, T. Hayward, R. Abel, W. Lockwood, J.T. Tyldesley; front: W. Rhodes,
J. Gunn.

invested by the county for his family in the future. Though well-intentioned and, in a number of cases, quite justified, it was not popular with those who considered themselves able to run their own affairs.

In general the professionals had little scope for any action to advance grievances without risking dismissal. The most significant such incident occurred just prior to the Third and final Test against Australia at The Oval in 1896. Five of the professionals due to play – George Lohmann, Tom Richardson, Bobby Abel and Tom Hayward of Surrey and William Gunn of Nottinghamshire – sent a letter to the Surrey committee, the relevant section of which read: 'We the following players having been asked to represent England v. Australia on August 10 and two following days do hereby take the liberty to ask for increased terms viz. twenty pounds. The importance of such fixture entitles us to make this demand.'

The Surrey committee certainly thought it *was* a liberty. The players were brusquely told to accept the usual fee of £10 plus expenses or lose their places in the side. Abel, Richardson and Hayward gave in and played, Lohmann and Gunn lost their places. Their cause was not in vain, however, for two years later the Test match fee was doubled to £20.

What the professionals had not specified in their letter was that their grievance was not purely the amount of money they were paid, but threefold. In addition, they objected to the irregularities they believed to take place over the amounts paid to some amateurs, and to the disproportionate amount of money the Australians – all playing as amateurs –

made out of the Tests, sharing as they did a large percentage of the gate money. As far as the amateurs were concerned the two names mentioned most frequently were W.G. Grace and A.E. Stoddart. The objections had definite effect, for not only did the Surrey committee take the unprecedented step of making an announcement about what Grace was paid, on the first morning of the match, but A.E. Stoddart was so put out that he stood down and did not play.

On the subject in general, and especially regarding the Australians, the players had many allies – some of them with great influence, as *The Times* went some way to demonstrating in a leading article.

> The professionals, if they have erred in their method of ventilating what is certainly a grievance, have brought the subject of their cricket remuneration very prominently before the public. There has long been a strong feeling that the rates of payment should be revised since the 'gates' and general profits of matches in these last ten years have so enormously increased; and the discontent is no longer hidden since the professionals see the amount of money the Australians are making in their tour of England.

Having gone on to make the point of the varying wealth of the counties – pointing out Surrey's good fortune in having The Oval at a peppercorn rent from the Duchy of Cornwall – the 'Thunderer' does close the article more in the manner that might be expected. 'Loyalty to the Surrey club and patriotism for English cricket should have been a sufficient incentive to the players to have practised self-denial a while longer.'

In *The Players* Ric Sissons concludes that, 'In the context of the major contribution the professionals made to popularising cricket as a national institution they were undervalued and underpaid.' If this was true to some extent, given the standards and attitudes of the time and the poverty of the rest of the working class, they achieved a surprising progress both in terms of their earnings and conditions of employment – especially when compared to the lack of progress which followed.

In 1912 Nottinghamshire professionals received £3 per week summer pay for 20 weeks and winter pay of £1 per week for 32 weeks. They received home and away match fees of £5 and £6 respectively. They also received varying amounts of talent money and win money and a season ticket to travel from home to Trent Bridge. Not only after the First World War but over thirty years later, in 1945, their summer pay had not changed, winter pay had gone up to £2 and home and away match fees had gone up to £9 and £11 respectively. Neither talent money nor win money amounts had increased substantially. In the same vein, while only seven men gained benefits of over £2,000 before 1914, only another seven managed £2,500 between 1914 and 1945. The highest, Roy Kilner's in 1925, only got £300 more than George Hirst had done 21 years earlier in 1904. More telling was the fact that they were both Yorkshiremen.

Such evidence points to the Edwardian era as the time when the professional cricketer established himself to a remarkable degree and made more significant progress than he was ever to manage again until after the end of the distinction from amateurs and with the commercialism of the modern era.

5

AMATEUR STYLE

Neville Cardus often allowed his imagination and sentiments to get the better of him when writing about the Edwardian era, but amongst the purple prose there are regular pieces of incisive commentary, none more relevant than one in *Cricket* (1930). 'The priceless contribution of the public schools to cricket as a national game has been skilful and cultivated youth.' In one short sentence he encapsulated the essence of Edwardian amateurism. It did not exist before the period and did not survive beyond 1914.

Above everything else it was the youth of the amateurs which accounted for the manner in which they played and their attitude to cricket. Many of them started playing as soon as they left school, and one in three had finished their careers while they were still 25. Stanley Jackson was 22 when he first played for England against Australia; Ranji

BACK NUMBERS.—PRINCE RANJITSINHJI.

Ranji, sketched at the dinner given for him in the Guildhall, Cambridge in recognition of his achievements during the 1896 season.

was 23. Jackson scored 91 in his first innings and a century in his third, Ranji scored 62 in his first and 154 in his second – an innings described by H.S. Altham as one which 'no other batsman in the world could have played'. Precocious it may have been, but it was also refreshing and exciting and spectators loved it.

The flowering of this talent was greatly assisted by the importance attached to cricket at all public schools and the prestige of schools cricket as part of the national game. This combination meant that a schoolboy with any natural aptitude for the game could be guaranteed to be coached to the highest standard he was likely to attain, while at the same time often getting the opportunity to play in crucial matches at major grounds in front of large audiences. Each season at Lord's there was a succession of schools matches: Clifton v. Tonbridge, Rugby v. Marlborough, Cheltenham v. Haileybury, Beaumont v. The Oratory and Eton v. Harrow. Eton v. Harrow was to some extent in a league of its own, but a good example of the importance allotted to schools cricket was given by *The Times* in 1895. The paper's coverage of the match both headed the 'Sporting Intelligence' and dominated it to the tune of well over a column. George Lyttelton was at the match

A portrait by 'Spy' of R.A.H. 'Mike' Mitchell, the
devoted tutor of precocious cricket talent at Eton.

Reggie Spooner captaining the Marlborough side of 1899, a few weeks before he made the Lancashire début that so enraptured Cardus.

for the first time in his life and, probably encouraged by the sight of a waiter who had an apoplectic fit at the back of his father's box, he and his brother thought that they were 'seeing life'. Two days later when Archie MacLaren played his historic innings of 424 at Taunton the match was barely given three inches and was not even the lead story.

The quality of the school's intake notwithstanding, the strength of Eton was largely a result of the devotion of R.A.H. Mitchell, who was master-in-charge of cricket from 1866 until 1897. During the Edwardian period Eton produced 24 players for county cricket – many more than any other school – including seven captains. 'Mike', as he was known to everyone, could have claimed to be the outstanding university cricketer, but rather than continuing his career, as soon as he finished at Oxford, where he had the unique distinction of being captain for three years, he returned to Eton to devote himself to the school's cricket. He produced batsmen who were orthodox and yet attacking, who played properly and yet adventurously, qualities which became the hallmarks of amateur batting. To a generation of boys, the majority of whom were naturally self-assured, such an approach to cricket was almost instinctive.

In the circumstances it was divine justice that the most delightful product of the public schools was not an Etonian. Reggie Spooner was educated at Marlborough and

Spooner at the wicket later in his career; neat, relaxed and unmistakably an amateur.

while still at school demonstrated the elegance which made him pre-eminent among the stylists. By all accounts his batting reflected his character. His father was the Archdeacon of Liverpool, where an ecclesiastical upbringing and the contact that it brought with Liverpool, where great wealth rubbed shoulders with extreme poverty, encouraged Reggie's courteous charm. His son remembers that he was so modest that all he learnt about his father's cricketing deeds was by reading and from what other people told him. To George Lyttelton he was 'one of the nicest people I have ever known'. Most revealing about his batting were the comments of two professional bowlers, Charlie Blythe, who once said after Spooner had stroked a ball away through the covers, 'Mister Spooner, I would give all my bowling to make a shot like that,' and J.T. Hearne who said, 'To bowl at Mister Spooner was a pleasure, an honour and a privilege.'

Like many schoolboys who went on to greater heights, Spooner first made his mark at Lord's, playing for Marlborough against Rugby. In 1898, aged 17, he scored 139, then the following season, by this time captain of Marlborough, he scored 62 and 198. Within a few weeks of leaving school he made his first appearance for Lancashire, again at Lord's, against Middlesex, and this match provides the introduction for the most evocative pen-portrait Cardus ever wrote, *Batsmanship of Manners*.

> In the summer of 1899 a schoolboy walked to the wicket at Lord's to begin a Lancashire innings against Middlesex; with him was Albert Ward. He was a graceful young cricketer, and a little tuft of hair stood up on the crown of his head. His flannels seemed soft and billowy. This boy – his name was R.H. Spooner – was making his first appearance in county cricket in his summer holidays, fresh from Marlborough. It would be hard to imagine a severer ordeal for anybody, a trial in the sacrosanct air of Lord's, the searching eyes of the pavilion on you, MacLaren your captain, and one of the bowlers against you Albert Trott at his best, spinning and curving and dipping the ball astonishingly.
>
> R.H. Spooner that day made 83, an innings full of strokes that seemed to ripple over the grass, light and lovely as sunshine. Straight from the playing fields of Marlborough he came and conquered – nay, the word conquered is too hard and aggressive for Spooner; he charmed and won our heart and the hearts of his opponents.

Fact or fiction, it is Cardus at his best, and never did his subject better deserve such prose.

It was to be a fleeting introduction for shortly afterwards Spooner left England to fight in the Boer War – where he was wounded – and did not return to county cricket until 1903. During that season he showed that his batting had lost none of its quality. As well as registering his highest score of 247 against Nottinghamshire (at the time the highest score they had been subjected to) he scored 168 out of a first-wicket partnership with MacLaren for Lancashire of 368 (still a record for the county). But landmarks such as these were of secondary importance for Spooner, compared to the style of his batting and of each individual stroke, made in unhurried manner with consummate timing and using his wrists so that with a flash, or a more gentle flick, the ball was rapidly dispatched. His slight figure seemed almost frail and he rarely appeared to hit the ball hard – an illusion to which many fielders were sharply awakened.

It was another Lancastrian by birth, Lionel Palairet, whose name has most often been linked with Spooner's for elegant batsmanship. But if Spooner was blessed with a charisma of delicacy Palairet's was altogether more stately. The contrast was first presented by appearance, Palairet was tall with a splendid moustache and an aristocratic,

Lionel Palairet, an aristocrat among batsmen.

The Oxford side of 1892, captained by Palairet, with C.B. Fry one of its junior members. Standing: V.T. Hill, C.B. Fry, J.B. Wood, T.S.B. Wilson; seated: W.H. Brain, M.M. Jardine, L.C.H. Palairet, G.F.H. Berkeley, T.B. Case; front: R.T. Jones, F.A. Phillips.

high-boned face. He always wore a Harlequins cap. His batting gave H.S. Altham his first cricket thrills when, as a boy, he used to watch at Taunton during his summer holidays.

> Of all the great batsmen I have been privileged to watch and admire, none has ever given me quite the sense of confident and ecstatic elation as did Palairet in those days . . . A perfect stance, an absolutely orthodox method, power in driving that few have equalled and withal, a classic grace and poise, unruffled even in adversity.

No wonder he gave Altham a feeling of confidence: one day at The Oval he opened the Somerset innings against Surrey with three straight drives to the boundary in Tom Richardson's opening over.

C.B. Fry, not often one to admit inspiration from elsewhere when discussing his own talents, went some way towards doing so regarding his schooldays at Repton, where Palairet captained the XI. 'I evolved such cricket as I achieved from watching Lionel Palairet play . . .' He continues in a more familiar vein, 'and from my own inner nature – mostly the latter.' Fry also gives an interesting insight into the privileges some young aspiring amateurs were afforded: during the Easter holidays Palairet's father used to engage professionals – one of whom was the unfailingly accurate William Attewell of

Nottinghamshire — to bowl at Lionel and his younger brother Richard. The father's ambitions were amply repaid, and on two notable days in 1895 and 1896 the brothers scored hundreds together in partnerships for Somerset.

Palairet's early cricket development saw uninterrupted success as both schoolboy and undergraduate, from four seasons in the XI at Repton to four seasons as a blue at Oxford, and captain for the last two. While still an undergraduate he first played for Somerset just as the county was being admitted to first-class status. In the succeeding years Palairet was one of the most forceful demonstrations that they deserved their elevation. In 1892 he and H.T. Hewett established a world record partnership of 346 — scored in 210 minutes — but the home crowd at Taunton chiefly delighted in his driving out of the ground, either into the River Tone along one side or into the churchyard of neighbouring St James's at one end.

Spooner and Palairet were the two quintessential amateur Edwardian batsmen. As well as their style, in neither case would a cursory look at their figures give an inkling of their ability. Both could only afford the time to play regularly for their counties for a few seasons. While neither played many matches for England they were both assured of a place for the Gentlemen. Almost invariably in any analysis of the quality of batsmanship during the period their names are a yardstick by which others are judged.

Among the handful of amateurs — half a dozen at most — who automatically commanded a place in the England side during their careers, one, F.S. Jackson — 'Jacker' to most of his contemporaries — reserved his most heroic exploits, as batsman, bowler and captain, for the Test arena. And heroic they often were, for few players have so regularly stemmed the tide of a batting collapse with a resounding innings or made a vital bowling breakthrough, to say nothing of his captaincy decisions which at times seemed infallible. With the possible exception of W.G. Grace, Jackson's record and reputation leave him as the outstanding Test-playing amateur of any generation.

It was inevitable that such a figure as Stanley Jackson would appear among the ranks of Edwardian cricketers. His background was the epitome of Victorian prosperity reaping its rewards in Edwardian establishment and eventual ennoblement. His grandfather was a relatively humble leather merchant and tanner whose Leeds business lurched from one financial disaster to the next. Jackson's father brought an end to this instability and made the business into a highly profitable concern. Financially secure, he turned his attention to public affairs. From his first steps as a Leeds councillor he progressed to membership of Parliament, where he was recorded by the *Dictionary of National Biography* as being, 'a more than usually silent M.P.', a place in Lord Salisbury's Conservative cabinet and finally, in 1902, a peerage as the first Lord Allerton.

Stanley Jackson himself combined his cricket career with business, politics, military and imperial service, and succeeded at all of them. After serving in the Boer War he emerged as a colonel at the age of 30. His political career and service in India as Governor of Bengal (where, after he survived attempted assassination by an Indian girl who fired five shots at him, he remarked, 'Lucky she didn't have enough for a full over') brought him a knighthood, membership of the Privy Council and the highest award of the two Indian decorations: Grand Cross of both the Star of India and the Order of the Indian Empire.

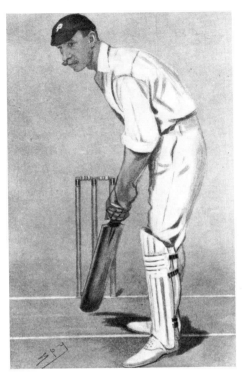

Stanley Jackson by 'Spy'. He was the best amateur all-rounder of the period and a figure of immense prestige.

Within two generations the rough corners had been smoothed away, and from an early age Stanley Jackson was unmistakably upper-class. At Harrow his fag was Winston Churchill – four years his junior – an association which was revived many years later when both men were Members of Parliament. Shortly after Jackson's arrival as a Unionist member, Churchill (at the time still a Liberal) introduced him to Lloyd George who exclaimed his delight on discovering Jackson's identity, 'I have been looking all my life for the man who gave Winston a hiding at school.'

If Churchill did get the occasional hiding it would have been well deserved because Jackson was neither harsh nor easily roused. His demeanour on the cricket field was immaculate and utterly self-assured, but quietly so, with little fuss, as was expected from a gentleman. Beneath his impassive exterior there was no question about Jackson being competitive – he demonstrated that during his second year as Cambridge's captain in 1893 when he ordered C.M. Wells to bowl wides to prevent Oxford following-on – but the outward signs were minimal. He was also tenacious in a manner more often expected from professional players than dashing amateurs, but it was this element of commitment which was so often decisive in his performances for England.

After his emphatic début against Australia in the first two Tests of 1893, Jackson missed the last Test of the series because Lord Hawke would not release him from the Yorkshire side. Thereafter he appeared in every Test against Australia on their next four visits and it is in these matches that his star shone most brightly. As a batsman he was supremely adaptable: when Grace dropped him down the order to seventh in his second Test he scored a hundred, and on the only occasion he went in number one for England he did the same. He batted at every position from one to seven, usually in the middle order, and demonstrated a consummate ability to play whatever innings was demanded. Like most of his contemporaries he was at his best on the attack, but in 1902, when the weather was relentlessly bad, he emerged as England's most secure batsman.

Finally, in what proved to be his last series, in 1905, he took on the England captaincy – from Archie MacLaren, who had been one year his junior at Harrow. Jackson had been offered the captaincy previously to lead tours to Australia, but he was never able to commit the time to spend a whole winter away. It says much for his leadership qualities that the volatile MacLaren – who had already suffered a blow to his pride when he was passed over in favour of Plum Warner to lead the 1903–04 tour to Australia – was more than happy to play under him, which he had not been prepared to do in Warner's case.

The year 1905 was the zenith of Jackson's career. He won the toss in all five Tests, won the series 2–0 with three matches drawn, and headed England's batting and bowling averages. By the end of Australia's tour their luckless captain Joe Darling found time for a bit of humour at Scarborough, when he was due to toss with Jackson for the seventh time in the season. He appeared stripped to the waist and suggested that the decision should be made by 'tossing' in the manner he knew best – by wrestling. Jackson's response showed that he was not short of humour himself: he suggested that on this occasion the diminutive George Hirst deputize for him against the well-built Australian. In the Tests Jackson scored 144 in front of his home crowd at Headingley, and followed it with a second century in the next Test which made him the first – and only – man to score five hundreds against Australia in England. Thereafter he played a few matches for Yorkshire in 1906 and 1907 before retiring completely while still in his prime.

Jackson never captained Yorkshire – Lord Hawke was always at the helm – and therefore was one of the few players to have captained England but not his county. He only managed one full season, in 1898, when he confirmed his all-round ability with 1,500 runs and 100 wickets. For nearly twenty seasons he was the best amateur all-rounder in England and, by virtue of his appearance, his style of play and his personality, one of cricket's most distinguished ornaments.

Stanley Jackson was the youngest of seven children, but as five of the others were girls there was little likelihood that cricket would be a family affair. About the same time in the West Country, however, it was a different story. The Reverend Henry Foster, a housemaster at Malvern College, had seven sons and they all played for Worcestershire. Their collective prowess was largely responsible for the county's elevation to first-class status in 1899, when three were in the side and the eldest, H.K., was captain, but one of their number, Reginald Erskine or 'Tip', was, during his brief career, one of the most dazzling performers of the Edwardian era and described by Cardus as 'one of the three or four really great batsmen of the early 1900s'. The last years of his life were plagued by the onset of diabetes and he died in 1914 aged 36.

*'Fostershire': the Rev. Henry Foster with his seven sons who all played for
Worcestershire. R.E. and B.S. at the back; W.L. and H.K. in the middle and
M.K., N.J.A. and G.N. in the front.*

Foster went up to Oxford in 1897 and got the first of his four blues as a freshman. But it was not until his last season at university that he revealed his full ability in the most devastating fashion. Having become, in the early part of the season, only the second batsman to score hundreds in each innings of a match twice, he went to Lord's for the University Match and made 171 – at the time the highest score in the competition. Ten days later he returned to Lord's for his first appearances in Gentlemen v. Players and provided the cream of a memorable match by scoring 102 not out in the first innings and 136 in the second.

Foster made something of a habit of breaking records in his first appearances in major competitions. Travelling to Australia as a member of Warner's 1903–04 side, he went in to bat in the First Test at Sydney and celebrated his Test début by scoring 287, which remained the highest Test score for nearly thirty years and is still the highest score by any player in his first Test.

Foster's batting was amateur style at its best. With a faultless array of strokes he had few equals at the cover drive and late cut, and hit the ball with dynamic power – in his two hundreds for the Gentlemen in 1900 he scored 156 of his 238 runs in fours, and in the same season he had the audacity to hit W.G. Grace for four consecutive sixes when batting for Oxford against the Old Man's London County side. He demonstrated the consistency he was capable of in 1901, his only full season for Worcestershire, when he scored over 2,000 runs at an average of 50, but his great gift was the ability to capitalize on his opportunities in a short career often interrupted for long periods by his business commitments. Time and again he came out for Worcestershire without having played for months and produced a sparkling innings, not least in 1905 when he scored 246 not out against Kent and in 1910, four years before his death, when he only played once and scored 133 against Yorkshire.

Of all English cricketers of the period – or rather, in this case, cricketers who played for England – only one has been frequently described as magical: Ranjitsinhji. To a nation obsessed with its imperialism and in the light of the strange ambivalent relationship which existed between England and India, Ranji was a source of fascination at the same time as exemplifying many of the curiosities of the Anglo–Indian balance. While he did not find it in the least unusual that an Indian should play cricket for England, neither did the majority of English observers. Rather the opposite: they were proud that an Indian prince should do so because it reflected well on British India and all it stood for. Ranji personified the element of the exotic which Englishmen knew was part of their empire but had not previously been found at home, and in that alone he added incalculably to the richness of cricket's flavour.

When Ranji first came to England enthusiasm was the most obvious feature of his cricket as well as a natural deftness best seen in his slip fielding. The enthusiasm was one of Ranji's most endearing qualities and stemmed not so much from a hearty enjoyment of sport but more from a keenness to please which a family background and childhood of dynastic in-fighting had produced. Modest, courteous and happiest when entertaining, either with his cricket or the lavish hospitality which he frequently dispensed, despite never having the funds to do so, Ranji won over the English crowds as much by dint of his personality as his prowess.

It was at Cambridge that the transformation in his cricket took place, from an obvious but untutored natural skill to mastery and ingenuity. Within a short time of arriving in England from India aged 16, Ranji had determined that cricket was his first love and ambition. Having acquired sufficient knowledge of the game's finer points, he set about ironing out the weaknesses and inconsistencies in his own game, assisted by the leading professional bowlers of the day. His dedication was inexhaustible. On one occasion when Stanley Jackson – who picked him to play for Cambridge in 1893 – found him in the nets and asked why he stayed there practising for so long, Ranji replied, 'I find I am alright for half an hour but I cannot last. I must now master endurance.'

It paid off. Having missed playing for Cambridge in 1894, forced to leave early because of a brief skirmish between the warring factions at home in Nawanagar, Ranji left to join Sussex. Here he could develop his friendship with C.B. Fry, begun when the two had opposed each other in the 1893 University Match, but also, as Alan Ross writes in his biography of Ranji: 'He had taken a liking to the place and the players. Brighton, with its Regency architecture and raffish crowds, its racegoers and rakes, gamblers and bucks, its sparkling sea air, seems absolutely right as a background for Ranji and he must have sensed it.'

Ranji at the wicket; a stance of easy, almost nonchalant orthodoxy.

Ranji's first season for Sussex in 1895 was a revelation. He scored over 1,700 runs but, more importantly, he batted in a manner which simply had never been seen before. He mesmerized bowlers and crowds alike, most famously with his late cut and leg glance, the latter stroke developed from batting for hours in the nets at Cambridge with his right foot pegged to the ground to improve his defence. As he became more consistently successful so he grew in confidence and was able to demonstrate his own batting dictum, 'Find out where the ball is; get there; hit it.' By the end of the season he was no longer a curiosity but a celebrity.

The 1895 season was the prelude to a flood of scintillating and record-breaking run-scoring over the next six seasons which was only interrupted by Ranji's health and affairs at home in India. Never robust, he found the English climate unfriendly to one brought up in the heat of India, and he suffered from appalling bouts of asthma. He missed the whole of the 1898 season which he spent in India. Not that he was idle when ill-health forced periods of inactivity. If *The Jubilee Book of Cricket* is anything to go by (which he conceived and produced, with the help of friends and experts, during a period of several weeks' illness in the 1896–97 winter), when he was not playing cricket he spent much of the time thinking about it.

Such was the reputation that Ranji had established during 1895, to say nothing of the public warmth he had generated, that the MCC's decision in 1896 not to include him in the team for the First Test against Australia was vociferously criticized. Lancashire redressed the situation by including him for the Second at Old Trafford, where Ranji repaid the decision handsomely. He scored 62 and 154 and completely outshone all other batsmen, English and Australian alike. By the end of the season he had overhauled W.G. Grace's record aggregate which had stood since 1871 by scoring 2,780 runs, and had equalled the Old Man's record ten centuries of the same year.

Ranji's climax came at the end of the century, in 1899 and 1900, when he amassed totals of 3,159 and 3,065 runs in the two seasons. He had proved that he was no mere 'bird of passage', as Lord Harris had feared he would be at the beginning of 1896, and installed himself as both the undisputed premier batsman in England and the successor to W.G. (as much as anyone would be able to take on his mantle) as the most charismatic personality in the game. If the beginning of the new century saw a slight falling away it was rather a question of Ranji returning to the levels of more mortal cricketers, although he did falter during the Tests of 1902 and dropped out of the side after the Second Test. At the end of the 1903 season he gave up the captaincy of Sussex which he had held since 1899, and 1904 was his last full season. Returning to India in the winter, at last, in 1907, he succeeded as Jam Saheb of Nawanagar and, other than a few fleeting visits, his cricket life in England had come to an end.

To come and go within the space of a decade or so and yet to leave such an indelible impression upon English cricket was the stuff of dreams and oriental magic which many of Ranji's contemporaries dwelt upon at the time, and others have done ceaselessly since. Descriptions and analyses of Ranji's batting are legion and varied, ranging from the Yorkshire brevity of his contemporary Ted Wainwright, 'Ranji! 'e never made a Christian stroke in his life,' to the more romantic Cardus, 'Happy the man who can close his eyes and see again the vision of Ranji, his rippling shirt of silk, his bat like a yielding cane making swift movements which circled round those incomparable wrists.' As perceptive as any was Ranji's biographer, Alan Ross:

> Yet for all the huge scores he made, Ranji never batted for the mere sake of it; nearly always he scored at about a run a minute, and while he was in he always put on some kind of display, each innings an expression of personality, an expression in technical skills, a series of experiments. He set out to demonstrate the most that could be achieved in certain conditions, consciously wanting to enchant as much as to dominate.

Ranji would have stood alone in any era, but it happened that his personal achievements were further elevated by the partnership which he established for Sussex with C.B. Fry. Cardus called it 'the occult and the rational', and without doubt it was one of the great features of the age which brought the crowds flocking to the seaside ground at Hove. It was a partnership of opposites, but no less productive for that. Whereas Ranji was retiring and always conscious of being something of an outsider, however much he was fêted and acclaimed, Fry suffered from no such inhibitions. No one had a higher opinion of his indisputable all-round genius than Fry himself, and throughout his life he remained strangely self-conscious for one so gifted. When he was the top Wadham Scholar at Oxford the fact that gave him his greatest satisfaction was that he beat F.E. Smith – the future Lord Birkenhead and Lord Chancellor of England. As far as his cricket was concerned, he bitterly resented any aspersions which were cast, in particular that he was not a natural player, that he was only inspired to greatness by his association with Ranji and that he had an illegal bowling action. The last rendered him almost apoplectic.

In the event, his bowling action apart, any discussion of Fry's cricketing ability was rendered academic by both his performance and his figures. Applying his intellect to the technique of batting, he evolved an almost infallible defence and formidable powers of attack, especially off the back foot and with the straight drive. In 1899 he topped 2,000 runs in a season for the first of six successive years and in 1901 even outstripped Ranji by topping the averages with an aggregate of 3,147 runs and an average of over 70. In that year he made thirteen hundreds, six of them in successive innings at the end of the season, a record which stood for nearly forty years until equalled by the insatiable Bradman.

It was as much his appearance at the wicket as his deeds with the bat which was memorable about Charles Fry, and eulogies about his classical 'Grecian' good looks were carried to fanciful heights by H.S. Altham who once wrote that he could have 'stepped straight out of the frieze of the Parthenon'. Like many of his contemporaries he appears from the distance of nearly a century to have been larger than life to a degree that could only have been accommodated in the Edwardian era when, as John Arlott wrote, 'an unusually large number of outstandingly gifted men who, encouraged by the circumstances and temper of the time, applied their gifts to sport, lifting it to new heights and making themselves the first generation of sporting idols'.

Of all Edwardian amateurs there was one for whom style was probably the least

Less orthodox, but no less effective: 'the Croucher' Gilbert Jessop in an equally characteristic position.

applicable description of his mode of batting, but in terms of scoring runs at an electrifying rate there has never been an equal to Gilbert Jessop. No professional would ever have dared to take the risks which Jessop took at the wicket, and if he curbed some of his youthful impetuosity to the extent of refraining from charging out and swiping at every ball, he was never restrained for long. As W.G. Grace's long career with Gloucestershire was coming to an end, Jessop took over as the county's major attraction, and if he scored at less than a run a minute it was – by his standards – a dull innings. As he demonstrated in his legendary innings of 104 in 77 minutes in the final Test of 1902 at The Oval which enabled England to pull off an impossible victory, Jessop had no equal as a batsman able to rouse a crowd to a frenzy of excitement. He was the supreme entertainer, as H.S. Altham explained when he described Jessop as 'the living embodiment of that sensationalism which will always make the most direct and compelling appeal to the man who pays his shilling and wants his money's worth'.

In *A History of Cricket* Altham also gave a masterly description of Jessop's batting which conveys a vivid impression of his explosive ability.

> As a hitter, Jessop stands absolutely alone; others, such as C.I. Thornton and Bonnor, may have driven the ball farther and higher, but no cricketer that has ever lived hit it so often, so fast, and with such a bewildering variety of strokes. His very stance, like a panther's crouch bespoke aggression. The secret of his hitting lay in his speed, of eye, of foot and of hand. He combined in a unique degree strength and flexibility of shoulder, arm and wrist. Length had no meaning for him; it was the length ball he hit best, and he hit it where the whim or the placing of the field suggested. One moment he would drive it along the ground or lift it, straight or with pull, over the deep-field's head; the next he would drop on his right knee and sweep the off-ball round to square leg, or lie back and cut it like a flash past third man. It was impossible to keep him quiet, impossible to set a field for him. When he was in form, the best bowlers were as helpless against him as the worst; he hit them just where and when he pleased.

Effective though he undoubtedly was, Jessop's unorthodoxy caused him to be regarded with mixed feelings, almost as something mercurial, by the powers in English cricket, and as a result his Test career was limited to few matches. MacLaren, himself a gambler and adventurer, would have always played him, but the more sober Stanley Jackson considered him a potential risk and the senior statesmen – Lords Harris and Hawke – agreed with Jackson. Therefore when Jessop first appeared for England, in the Second Test of 1899, he was chosen as the team's only fast bowler, but he scored 50 in a partnership with Jackson which halted a headlong collapse in the first innings.

The fact that Jessop originally played for England as a fast bowler emphasizes the degree to which he was an all-rounder, completed by his lightning speed in the field. One of the few amateurs who was in the same class as an all-rounder was J.N. Crawford, whose career was frustratingly cut short by a disagreement with his county, Surrey. Cricket was certainly in Crawford's blood, as his father and uncle and two brothers all played for counties. But from an early age he was clearly going to be the family star – indeed a schoolboy prodigy.

J.N. Crawford when he was enthralling crowds at
The Oval during his all-too-short career with Surrey.

Such was his success at Repton that, aged 17, he was picked to play for Surrey during the summer holidays, and ended the season topping the county's bowling averages and being second in the national ones with 44 wickets at a cost of just under 17 runs apiece. Having returned to Repton for his last year, he rejoined Surrey for the end of the 1905 season and then toured South Africa in the winter. A year later he went to Australia and headed England's bowling averages with 30 wickets taken on flawless wickets, and even the great Sydney Barnes had to take second place to the 21-year-old.

It was in England, during his brief career with Surrey, that he demonstrated his all-round ability, doing the double of 1,000 runs and 100 wickets in 1906 – becoming the youngest cricketer to do so, which he remained for over forty years – in 1907, and just missing it in 1908. As a batsman he was an unforgettable sight, for he was one of the first cricketers to play in spectacles, but this did not impair his considerable hitting power which was adored by spectators at The Oval during his few years at Surrey, as described by *The Times* in the paper's description of Crawford in full flight scoring a century in 1907: 'Nervous people had mounted to the roof stand to be out of the way of the ball, but Crawford found them with one tremendous overhead drive which scattered them in all directions.'

Alas, it was all too short. In 1909 Crawford was asked to deputize in a match against the Australians for the regular Surrey captain, H.D.G. Leveson-Gower, whose diminutive stature earned him the nickname 'Shrimp', but who was later to become a pillar of cricket's establishment and to be knighted for his services to the game. Crawford objected when three players whom he considered crucial were left out, and in the end refused to captain the side for the game. After a short lull the wrath of the authorities descended upon his head when he refused to accede to the demands of the Surrey president, Lord Alverstone, to apologize to Leveson-Gower. Thereafter Leveson-Gower wrote to the luckless Crawford informing him that on account of his behaviour he was withdrawing his invitation for Crawford to play in his side at Scarborough and that the MCC would not be considering him for the forthcoming tour to South Africa. Finally he was informed by Surrey that they no longer required his services. Crawford left England to live in Australia and, although he returned and actually played again for Surrey after the war, he was not the same youthful genius of twenty years earlier.

There is no doubt that it was ill-deserved treatment for the brightest amateur star Surrey had seen in years, and it was a grievous loss for them and English cricket in general – especially when one considers the studied opinion of H.S. Altham who was two years his junior at Repton, that he would have qualified for the Gentlemen as either a batsman or a bowler during his last two years at school.

One cannot help feeling that Crawford would not have been so readily lost if he had been a member of Lord Harris's Kent side, where amateur skill was deeply entrenched and highly prized. When the county won the championship in 1906 their batting averages were headed by five amateurs and, although it had been a desperate struggle to beat off Yorkshire, it was universally agreed that the win was well deserved on account of the quality of entertainment provided by the Kent side. The crucial and most attractive contribution was made by K.L. Hutchings, a young batsman of 23, whose career was perhaps the most poignant of all amateurs. During a few brief seasons he burst upon

K.L. Hutchings, Kent's most exhilarating batsman, in the
BB blazer that distinguished the county's amateurs.

English cricket and then, having left the game in 1912, was killed in action in 1916 aged 33. His ability and charm were captured by H.S. Altham:

> Hutchings had done brilliantly for Tonbridge, for which he played five years, and had played some good innings for Kent in 1903, but no one was prepared for his meteoric success three years later. He did not come into the eleven until mid-June, yet a month later he was picked for the Gentlemen at Lord's, and for a couple of months was widely regarded as the most brilliant amateur batsman playing.
>
> In style he was a thorough individualist; in defence he was a good back-player; but he will be remembered best for his driving. Blessed with abnormally strong wrists and forearms, the power of his straight and on-driving was really alarming, yet there was no spectacular effort on the stroke, only a lightning acceleration at the vital moment. As a fielder, whether in the slips or in the out-field, he was magnificent; with his crisp black hair, strong, athletic body and sparkling methods, he was the idol of Kent grounds.

Such short-lived and transient brilliance, with all its youthful zest and appeal, and the eventual premature demise, encapsulated both the quality and fate of Edwardian amateurism. Neither Hutchings nor half of his contemporaries would have left anything like the impression they did had they had to establish and then graft out their careers over fifteen or twenty seasons. Their contribution was one of sparkle, not stability, and inasmuch would always have a limited life. If only a proportion of them were actually killed in action, they would never again make a comparable contribution to English cricket as they did for two decades before 1914.

6

PROFESSIONAL SKILL

The young professional had few of the advantages of the schoolboy amateur. Making it to play for a county was usually as much a question of luck as of talent. The budding amateur had only to demonstrate ability to be ensured of steady upward progress to a stage where – if he so wished – he could play for a county. A young professional had to be noticed. If noticed, a junior post on the groundstaff at the county ground was the major step forward, but to progress from here to the supreme goal of a place in the county XI – and to retain that place – he had to show not only talent but the most essential professional quality: consistency. Consistency guaranteed his place and therefore a secure living. Given that this was the seemingly simple but all too often elusive goal for the Edwardian working class, its importance should not be underestimated. Certainly, however, the situation improved considerably throughout the period. As the status of a professional cricketer acquired respectability and recognition, so his position became less precarious.

Except in the cases of a handful of the top players, it was never guaranteed, and professionals could not afford the luxury of amateurs who, playing for enjoyment not a living, could bat with carefree style and either score runs or not. Similarly, bowlers were expected both to take wickets and to bowl for exhaustingly long spells. J.T. Hearne bowled over 2,000 overs when he topped the averages in 1896; when he was top again two years later he bowled 1,800. Wilfred Rhodes bowled over 3,000 overs when he was the leader in the two seasons of 1900 and 1901. In 1906, when George Hirst did his double of 2,000 runs and 200 wickets, no wonder he said afterwards that if anyone equalled it they would be very tired: as well as batting through 58 innings at an average of over 45, he bowled over 1,200 overs. No one has ever equalled it, and only two men have bowled more than 1,000 overs in a season during the last twenty years.

The fact that players were noticed at an early age and that professional talent did surface in county cricket confirmed the extent of the game's grass roots and the fact that by the 1890s it was an increasingly well-organized national institution. The majority of professional talent was spotted in club cricket and, in the north and midlands, in the leagues. According to *Wisden*, Bobby Abel was 'found in club cricket in Southwark Park'. Sydney Barnes caught the eye of Billy Ward, the professional with Smethwick, Barnes's home side in the Birmingham and District League. Ward taught Barnes how to bowl an off-break and steered him in the direction of Edgbaston where he had played his county cricket.

CRICKETERS IN THE FIELD.
ABEL.

Bobby Abel, who was 'found' playing club cricket and who went on to become one of the most popular and respected Edwardian professionals.

*Tom Hayward, Abel's successor as senior pro at The Oval
and the representative professional batsman.*

In many cases cricket was instilled at an early age by a devoted father. Sometimes it was in the blood. As well as the famous cricketing families such as the Gunns of Nottinghamshire and the Hearnes of Kent and Middlesex, a number of players benefited from the involvement of their fathers – or other relations – with the organized world of cricket. Before he ever came under scrutiny from Tom Hayward, Jack Hobbs was given his first introduction to cricket because his father was on the groundstaff at the Cambridge University ground, Fenner's, and subsequently – by the time Jack was a schoolboy – groundsman and umpire at Jesus College, Cambridge. Hobbs himself gives a revealing description of these formative days in his career.

At this time my father was the groundsman at Jesus College. I watched at the nets a lot, and practised strokes. The undergraduates in those days thought it stylish to use a good deal of flourish, in spite of which their underlying principle was the straight bat. I learned the value of the straight bat from them, though I eliminated the flourish, possibly because the bat was too heavy for my boyish arms to indulge in such feats. We boys used to play in front of the servants' quarters of the college. Our weapons would be a tennis ball with a tennis post as wicket, and a stump as bat. The 'pitch' was a gravel one. This scratch kind of cricket got me in the way of playing correct strokes and the stump-bat was certainly capital for training the eye.

In such a manner countless professionals first developed their skill.

The relationship between Tom Hayward and Jack Hobbs demonstrates the links and networks which led professionals from youthful obscurity to a place in a county side, the huge reputations of the top professionals and, in the difference between the two men, it illustrates the subtle changes in style and attitude which the twenty years of the Edwardian era brought about.

Tom Hayward was the archetypal professional and a stalwart of the Wilfred Rhodes 'cricket's not meant to be fun' school of thought. Cardus wrote that he 'could have batted in spats and a tall hat'. Born in Cambridge into a cricketing family – his uncle was one of the best batsmen of the mid-nineteenth century – who had moved from Surrey and had strong connections with The Oval, Tom journeyed thence with no illusions about what was required to succeed as a professional cricketer: hard work and consistency. Combining his talent with determination, he crafted a style of batting that was as foolproof as one could have hoped for. It was designed, as Philip Trevor commented, 'For the elimination of risk.' Trevor also describes how only very occasionally did Tom allow his batting any embellishments that could be construed as unnecessarily adventurous. 'Surrey were never quite safe, even when Tom had made over 200, but now and again, on the rare occasions when they could not lose, Thomas Hayward allowed himself to do a little "six"-hitting.'

Thus armed, he became the model of consistency. C.B. Fry called him a 'thoroughly reliable and imperturbable hero'. For most of the period the sight of his tall, slightly stooping figure, complemented by his full drooping moustache, walking out to open an innings inspired more confidence in Surrey and England supporters than any other, and he was unrivalled in his ability to dispel the threat of a fast bowling attack within the space of a few overs. One of only five players to appear in all twenty seasons from 1895 to 1914, he scored 1,000 runs in every one. In ten of them he scored 2,000 and twice – in 1904 and 1906 – going on to over 3,000, his 3,518 in 1906 remaining unequalled until 1947. He became the first batsman after W.G. to score 100 hundreds. Amateur and professional contemporaries alike were unanimous that he was the most reliable batsman of the period.

These achievements were all of the utmost importance in that they were a guarantee of security. They enabled Hayward to negotiate a long-term contract with Surrey and, after the retirement of Abel, Richardson and Lockwood, placed him in a pre-eminent position among the Oval professionals. When Surrey played away matches, supper-time in their hotel was similar to a scene in the servants' hall of a country house, Tom Hayward at the top of the table dispensing the food and the orders in the manner of an all-powerful butler. The youthful Herbert Strudwick, during his first days at The Oval, once strayed inadvertently onto the stairs leading to the senior professionals' dressing-room, where he met Hayward and was brusquely ordered downstairs to the juniors' room.

Senior professionals such as Tom Hayward had all the Victorian principles drummed into them at an early age, while, given the greatly increased reputation of cricket and its leading players during the Edwardian era, their authority grew correspondingly. There is no more concise indication of this authority than the 20-year-old Jack Hobbs's description of his journey from Cambridge to London in April 1903, having been

Hayward's youthful protégé, Jack Hobbs, who more than emulated the achievements of his mentor.

informed that he was to be given the trial for which he had been waiting all through the previous winter.

> In those days I would no more have thought of going up to Tom Hayward than I would have thought of going to see the King. So I waited until Tom sent for me. He told me how to go and what to do. I was to take the train to Liverpool Street, and on arriving at The Oval I was to ask for W.T. Grayburn, the Surrey coach.

Hobbs had idolized Hayward for many years and the ambition to emulate him as a batsman was the driving force of his early career. When in 1905, after two years' residence in the county, he was qualified to play for Surrey, he proved himself the natural successor to Bobby Abel, who had retired the previous year, as Hayward's opening partner. It was through this partnership that Hayward passed on his strict agenda for batting and life as a professional. Hobbs was made clearly aware of the need to succeed and that, as he said himself, 'unless you got to the top where the plums are, it is a bare living, and when your cricket days are over, you have to find a new career'.

Far from purely copying his mentor, Hobbs adapted the lessons to his own style of batting, and at the same time absorbed the more general influences of the Edwardian age such as the dash of many amateurs and the aspiration towards perfecting a complete range of strokes with which to dominate bowling on any wicket. By 1914, and the end of the first half of his career, he was already demonstrating that he possessed a greater degree of such all-round batting mastery than any other player with the possible exception of W.G. Grace. Confirmation came during the inter-war years when he overhauled most of Grace's batting records.

It is one of the most satisfying coincidences of cricket history that Jack Hobbs made his first-class début against a side captained by W.G. Grace in the twilight of the Old Man's career. The thread of continuity was symbolically cemented in this meeting when Grace, who had dominated the nineteenth century, bowed out to Hobbs who was to do likewise with the twentieth. It was in April 1905 when Hobbs was picked for Surrey against Grace's Gentlemen of England XI – for whom he was to play his last first-class game only three years later. The 22-year-old Hobbs scored 88 in his second innings and Grace, now 56, stroked his beard in thoughtful appreciation and remarked that he would become a 'good 'un'.

Grace's prediction was borne out with ever-increasing assurance. Only a fortnight after the two had met, Hobbs scored 155 in his first county match and was promptly awarded his county cap by the Surrey captain Lord Dalmeny. By the end of the season he had scored over 1,300 runs, a modest total by his future standards. Two years later he was chosen to tour Australia in 1907–08, ironically because Tom Hayward and others of the senior professionals had refused the terms offered and declined to go. He returned with his reputation as a batsman as good as assured and his place as England's opener equally secure, as it was to remain for over twenty years.

By the time Jack Hobbs had become established as one of the foremost cricketers of the day, many of the most illustrious Edwardian characters – batsmen such as Stanley Jackson and Ranji and bowlers such as Tom Richardson and Bill Lockwood – had either

Bill Lockwood (left) and Bobby Peel, masterly bowlers who both suffered through their weakness for the bottle.

*Johnny Tyldesley, one of the few professional batsmen who could command an
England place in preference to the array of amateurs.*

left the game or were only playing very occasionally. When the best of them were on
form and available, between 1899 and 1905, the only professional batsman other than
Tom Hayward who could regularly claim a place in the England side was J.T. Tyldesley of
Lancashire.

Johnny Tyldesley was born at Roe Green, near the town which shared his name just
west of Manchester. He learnt his cricket in the leagues but as soon as he joined
Lancashire, in 1895, he demonstrated that his natural game was far removed from the

dour competitive image of league cricket. The memory of a Lancashire innings opened by Reggie Spooner and Archie MacLaren, with Johnny Tyldesley going in first wicket down, made Neville Cardus go weak at the knees, and of the three, if Spooner was the most stylish and MacLaren the most impressive, Tyldesley was the most dynamic.

Lancashire had good reason to be proud of Tyldesley. At the time that he emerged into the county side they had built up something of a reputation for enticing their leading professionals from other counties. To have a home-bred player of Tyldesley's calibre was the perfect answer to such criticisms and he remained loyal to the county club for the rest of his life, becoming the coach at Old Trafford when he retired until a year before his death in 1930. One of his best pupils was his younger brother, Ernest.

Tyldesley was something of an enigma among his professional contemporaries in that he appeared to scorn caution and modesty of style. His small stature – he only stood 5ft 6ins – must have exaggerated his aggression and speed at the wicket, and he was a firm believer that bowling should be attacked. *Wisden* once carried a description of how, if forced to bat out a maiden over, he would stand at the crease chewing at the thumb of one glove with frustration. The worst wickets or most serious crises brought out the best in Tyldesley. Many contemporaries considered his innings of 62 out of a total of 103 on a rain-affected sticky wicket at Melbourne in 1903–04 the best of his career. In the First Test of the 1902 series, when England fielded what has often been regarded as their strongest batting line-up of any Test, Tyldesley was the only professional among the batsmen, going in at number five after MacLaren, Fry, Ranjitsinhji and Jackson. After MacLaren, Fry and Ranjitsinhji had been dismissed with the total at 35, Tyldesley scored 138. He was never one to be overawed by a surfeit of amateur brilliance.

In 1906 Tyldesley made the highest score of his career, 295 not out against Kent at Old Trafford. It was the highlight of a match notable otherwise for the first appearance in the Kent side of a tall 18-year-old all-rounder destined to become the county's outstanding cricketer and by common consent the most elegant of professional batsmen, Frank Woolley. George Lyttelton coupled him with Lionel Palairet and called them, 'the Ciceros of batsmanship'. After the First World War, Woolley's career continued almost until the outbreak of the Second, his last season for Kent being in 1938, and it was during the inter-war years that he established his reputation as one of the greatest of all-rounders. By even the highest professional standards his consistency was phenomenal: he scored 1,000 runs in 28 seasons and 2,000 in 13, combining this in four seasons with 100 wickets – a unique record. His aggregate of runs is second only to Hobbs and amongst those who have made 100 hundreds he is, with the possible exception of Grace and Hammond, the only one who could claim to be a bowler – which he was to the tune of more than 2,000 wickets. In addition he is the only player to have taken over 1,000 catches.

Only a few weeks after the match at Old Trafford, in his fourth match for Kent, Woolley went in to bat against Hampshire at Tonbridge with the score at 23 for three, and made a hundred 'in about an hour and a half', *Wisden* seemed to recall. The commentary continues laconically that 'the colt Woolley deserves more than passing notice'. Having been born in Tonbridge, Woolley had been noticed by the Kent authorities while still a schoolboy and introduced to the nursery at the Tonbridge

Frank Woolley at the time that Wisden *described him as*
'the colt'.

ground. In a county dominated by amateur batsmen, so that in the championship-winning year of 1906 the first five batsmen in the county averages were all amateurs, it was hardly surprising that the young débutant was impressionable, as he himself later admitted, saying that he realized that to succeed he would have to bat like the amateurs.

This only partially accounts for the unhurried grace of his batting. It was only possible in a left-hander who combined unusual height – and therefore reach – with consummate timing and an imperturbable nature. Equally important for Kent, his presence in the middle order of the batting brought both continuity and stability to complement the amateur sparkle which, brilliant when at its full strength, was often dependent upon the availability of the leading lights.

From his first appearance for Kent until 1914, Woolley established himself as an invaluable all-rounder but, as a bowler, he had to be content with second place to another slow left-armer quite different in build and temperament, Colin Blythe. 'Charlie' Blythe, as he was always called, was a melancholy, brilliant rarity among professionals of the Edwardian era. His great love was playing the violin, and his artistry, ill-health and sensitivity were totally unsuited to the demands made upon professional cricketers. An especially taxing spell of bowling could bring him close to breakdown, as occurred in 1907 when he won the Second Test at Leeds for England by taking 15 South African wickets for 99 and bowled almost unchanged throughout the match. At one stage his doctor recommended to the Kent committee that he did not play in Test matches, so great did he find the strain. He was born into a poor family in the inauspicious surroundings of Deptford where he was spotted playing a primitive schoolboy game by the indefatigable Captain McCanlis, the coach at the Tonbridge nursery. In his first game for Kent in 1899 Blythe bowled Frank Mitchell of Yorkshire with his first ball.

From then until 1914, despite all the problems of his health and temperament, he was a bowler of tenacity and deadly effect. On five different occasions he bowled unchanged through both innings of a match and on one day in 1907 he took 17 Northamptonshire wickets for 48 runs, a record for a day's play that has never been surpassed. Of the bowlers who have taken more than 2,000 wickets in their careers, only Tom Richardson did so in less than Blythe's 16 seasons. In Tests Blythe took 100 wickets in only 19 matches.

Transcending the number of wickets was the manner in which they were taken. H.S. Altham wrote that, 'to watch his mastery of flight and spin was an aesthetic experience'. The spin he generated on damp wickets made him almost unplayable and when the pitch offered no assistance he teased batsmen into errors with variations of flight and pace. There is no question that his bowling was the decisive factor in Kent's championship victories in 1906, 1909, 1910 and 1913. In an age when cricketing genius was so appreciated and admired, Blythe was regarded with huge affection by his playing contemporaries and when, in 1917, he was killed in action at Passchendaele, his death

'Charlie' Blythe, a sensitive and artistic anomaly among
Edwardian professionals.

Confidence, dedication and sense of purpose are all visible
in this portrait of Wilfred Rhodes.

was felt more deeply among cricketers than any other of the war years, with the possible exception of Victor Trumper.

With Blythe, the other great slow left-arm bowler of the period was Wilfred Rhodes, and a more different character would be hard to imagine. Even in Yorkshire, the citadel of professional cricket, Rhodes stood out. As if to atone for the misdemeanours of Bobby Peel, whose place as Yorkshire's slow left-armer he was chosen to fill, throughout his long career with the county Rhodes never acted or spoke in a manner that was not sober, at times sombre. Cricket was a serious business and there was no room for flights of fancy.

It was in Wilfred Rhodes that the Yorkshire cricketer of popular imagination was born: dour, competitive and difficult to impress, he went on relentlessly from season to season scoring runs and taking wickets with no fuss or bother. By the end of over thirty years with the county he had played in nearly 900 matches and had established unique all-round career figures which were a testament to devoted hard work: nearly 40,000 runs, over 4,000 wickets and the season's double of 1,000 runs and 100 wickets 16 times. For England he began batting at number eleven and advanced up the order until some ten years after his first Test he was opening the innings with Jack Hobbs. He gave as few chances to fielders when he was batting as he did to batsmen when he was bowling.

Rhodes's quality as a bowler was that he never gave the batsmen any respite and, especially for Yorkshire, his campaign of successive balls was conducted with military precision, forcing the batsman to play to his field. Cardus encapsulated it when he wrote:

> He prevailed by length, variations of flight, but chiefly by unceasing accuracy of pitch, always demanding close attention from the batsman, the curving arc through the air, the ball dropping on the same spot over by over, and yet not on quite the same spot, each over in collusion with the rest, every ball a decoy, some balls apparently guileless, some artfully masked – and one of them sooner or later the master ball. He was economical in action, a few short strides, then a beautifully balanced sideways swing of the body, the arm loose and making a lovely arch. He could go on for hours; the rhythm of his action was in its easy rotation, hypnotic, lulling his victims to a tranced state in which he could work his will, make them perform strokes contrary to their reason and intention.

Rhodes's personal achievements were amassed over the two periods of his career, but during the first – pre-war – period his reputation as an individual player was enhanced by his partnership with George Hirst. Both men were born in the village of Kirkheaton – Hirst the elder by some six years – just outside Huddersfield and about twenty miles from Headingley. For over a decade their opening attack, Hirst's fast-medium left-arm and Rhodes's slow left-arm was, if not as intimidating as some of the quicker bowlers', probably the most effective in the country.

George Hirst shared Rhodes's fierce competitiveness, but was a very different character to his henchman: short, squat and full of smiling energy, his bluntness usually sweetened with a joke. His bowling was equally effective, however, especially after he had begun to perfect the swing bowling which, novelty that it was, bamboozled so many batsmen. On one occasion when Yorkshire were playing at Cheltenham during the festival, word of Hirst's new method of attack had preceded him, and W.G. Grace forewarned one of his younger batsmen by advising him to go off and buy a 'box' to protect himself against Hirst's in-swinger. The unfortunate young man could only find one made of metal and when he went in to bat – with W.G. at the other end – proved unable to keep out Hirst's bowling. After a few balls W.G. compounded the poor youth's considerable embarrassment by calling down the wicket, 'I told you to get a box, not a musical box.'

As all-rounders, Hirst and Rhodes are on a pinnacle of their own, and if Rhodes's career figures are the greater, Hirst's 14 doubles of 1,000 runs and 100 wickets are on a par and his single double of 2,000 and 200 in 1906 never approached, while his 341 against Leicestershire in 1905 remains the highest score for Yorkshire. Such were the career achievements of Hirst and Rhodes, not only the factual and statistical, but also the legendary, such as their partnership against Australia at The Oval in 1902 when, after Jessop had made 102 in 75 minutes, Rhodes came in last to join Hirst with 15 needed and they scored the runs to win the match, that they have deservedly been described in superlatives.

At a time when the game enjoyed such a huge reputation Hirst and Rhodes exemplified professional skill at the highest level. They were the master craftsmen in a

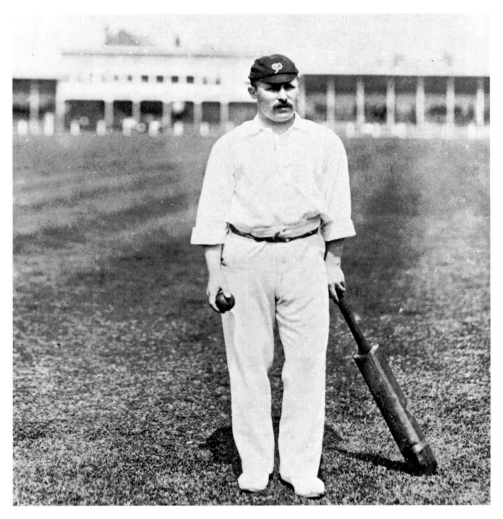

*Rhodes's henchman, George Hirst, the stocky all-rounder who in 1906 achieved
the never-equalled double of 2,000 runs and 200 wickets.*

Yorkshire side where professionalism was honed to perfection, and a force in the county
championship which no other side could match. In the twenty seasons from 1895 to 1914
Yorkshire were the winners eight times and only out of the top three in four seasons. As
interesting as their records was the fact that two such players appeared from the same
place within a few years of each other, which, as well as being a coincidence of nature, is
both a reflection upon the age and upon cricket in Yorkshire at that time, as *Wisden*
described in its obituary of George Hirst: 'The people of Kirkheaton and the surrounding
areas almost lived for cricket.'

Cricket was far more widespread as a working-class game in Yorkshire than, for instance, in neighbouring Lancashire, which partially explains Lancashire's comparative dearth of home-grown professionals, as Ric Sissons described in *The Players*:

The slower mechanisation in West Yorkshire and Nottinghamshire allowed semi-rural villages to survive and, as a by-product, produce professional cricketers. The significant difference between those two counties and Lancashire was that the cotton trade was rapidly mechanised and organised via factories from the 1840s. The newly-urbanised industrial working-class in Lancashire worked long hours and lived in towns and cities which lacked basic recreational activities and space. Consequently Lancashire failed to generate home-grown professional talent and resorted to importing players from Notts and Yorkshire. It should also be added that the best Lancashire club sides restricted their membership to the middle and upper classes via a two guinea subscription which a working man could not afford. In comparison the annual subscription with a good Yorkshire club was half a guinea or less.

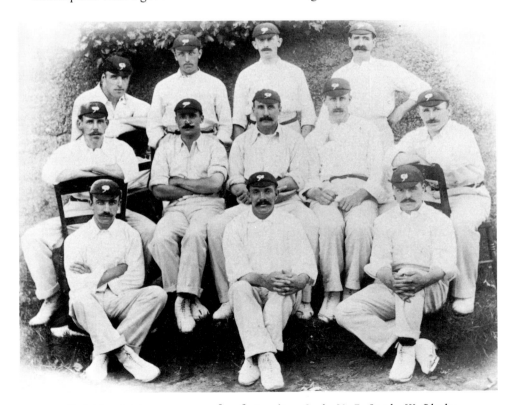

Yorkshire 1900: an armoury of professionalism. Back: Mr E. Smith, W. Rhodes, L. Whitehead, D. Hunter; middle: E. Wainwright, Mr T.L. Taylor, Lord Hawke, J. Tunnicliffe, G. Hirst; front: D. Denton, J.T. Brown, S. Haigh.

The cluster of towns in south-west Yorkshire was the catchment area for this professional strength. David Denton – who, like George Hirst, played in all twenty seasons, scored 1,000 runs in virtually all of them and was an equally brilliant fielder – came from near Wakefield; Schofield Haigh, who with Hirst and Rhodes completed Yorkshire's triumvirate of regular bowlers, came from Berry Brow, a few miles from Kirkheaton on the other side of Huddersfield; John Tunnicliffe, one of the regular opening pair, from near Pudsey, between Leeds and Bradford; and the forthright all-rounder Ted Wainwright from Tinsley. Of the few amateurs who played, three – Stanley Jackson, Tom Taylor and Ernest Smith – were all Leeds men, while Lord Hawke oversaw operations from his home a few miles to the east of the city. Recruits from the more rural Ridings to the north and east were very much the exception, Scarborough being the only cricket centre outside Leeds and the surrounding woollen towns.

If Yorkshire had one distinct area of recruitment so too did neighbouring Nottinghamshire: in the county's collieries. Some twenty miners played for Nottinghamshire between 1895 and 1914, and many of them worked down the pits each winter: 'Topsy' Wass who came from Sutton-in-Ashfield, Thomas Oates, born in D.H. Lawrence's home village of Eastwood, Joe Hardstaff who was born in Kirkby-in-Ashfield, and Edwin Boaler Alletson who lived on the Duke of Portland's estate at Welbeck which was surrounded by collieries. They were tough and combative cricketers with scant respect for the reputations of opponents, either amateur or professional and, if not quite on a par with their neighbouring Yorkshiremen, provided such a strong nucleus of players that throughout the period the only regular amateur was the captain, A.O. Jones, who commanded universal respect from his players by virtue of his batting and fielding and his enthusiasm.

Amongst the ranks of miners or sons of miners, Nottinghamshire boasted the only well-known eccentric among professional cricketers of the period, George Gunn. The nephews of William Gunn who had forged with Arthur Shrewsbury the best opening partnership of the preceding era, George Gunn and his brother John played over 1,000 matches for Nottinghamshire between them. George was still playing in his fifties when he and his son, George junior, batted together to both score hundreds in the same innings.

The style of Gunn's batting was inimitable and his performances were governed largely by mood. When he felt like scoring runs he had few equals in making it look easy, especially against fast bowlers whom he would advance towards, often taking two or three steps, and on bad wickets. But if his mood was otherwise he was as likely to block and then offer the simplest of chances – which he did on one occasion before returning to the pavilion and telling his captain Jones that it was 'too 'ot'. In a match against Yorkshire in 1913 he scored 132 in six hours in the first innings and so the Yorkshire players decided to stir him up about being a slow scorer. In the second innings he scored 109 in 75 minutes out of 129 for three. His best-known innings was in Australia in 1907. Gunn was in Australia for his health and was drafted into the England side for the First Test at the last minute. The situation obviously appealed to him for he marked his Test début with 119 in the first innings and 74 in the second – both top scores.

George Gunn was one of few professionals who dared to take any risks with his career

CRICKETERS IN THE FIELD.
GUNN.

William Gunn, uncle of George, who established the family's central position in their county's cricket.

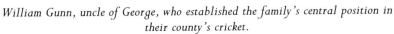

George Gunn, Nottinghamshire's eccentric genius.

by erratic behaviour, and he got away with it because of his natural skill as a batsman. He was also one of a select handful of senior professionals from the Edwardian era, which included Hobbs, Woolley and Rhodes, whose careers continued well into the inter-war period and who were able to give the younger generation an insight into the mixture of tough competitiveness, high standards and quality of play which had moulded them as young cricketers and which only survived the First World War in diluted form.

7

THE AUSTRALIANS

However buoyant the domestic game may have been, Edwardian cricket would have been immeasurably the poorer without the Australians, as visitors to England and as hosts to touring sides in their own country. They became the supreme opponents, motivated by a sporting ethos which was as tough and competitive – if not more so – than that in England. It is one of the more remarkable aspects of cricket history that while all other countries have taken decades from their introduction to Test cricket before being able to compete with England on equal terms, Australia were able to do so almost from the very start.

The 1880s and early 90s were the formative years of Test cricket. Its establishment was greatly encouraged by the regularity of series – 13 in as many years between 1880 and 1893. At the same time, however, the English sides visiting Australia were raised by individuals as privately organized tours and were never representative. This lack of full representation continued to be the case throughout the Edwardian era – although to a steadily lesser degree – when every touring English side still contained notable absences, in particular leading amateurs. Neither Stanley Jackson nor C.B. Fry ever toured Australia. But the organization became less speculative and eventually, for the 1903–04 tour, the MCC took over full responsibility for the visits.

The 1880s had ended on a low note for Australia, with lack of success by the players breeding lack of interest in the public. The 1891–92 tour, organized and financed by the magnanimous cricket-lover Lord Sheffield, did much to stop the rot, especially because his lordship brought the ultimate attraction in the form of W.G. Grace as captain, and because Australia managed to win 2–1. But the 1893 visit to England, led by J.M. Blackham on his eighth and final tour, whose captaincy and tour leadership were not in the same class as his wicket-keeping, was not a success, on or off the field. Then, in the winter of 1894–95, A.E. Stoddart led a very strong English side to Australia and won an outstanding series 3–2. As well as introducing to the Australians Archie MacLaren who became, over three visits, one of the most prolific of English batsmen on Australian wickets, and Tom Richardson, who bowled his heart out, for Australia the tour was of decisive significance and proved to be a perfectly timed stimulant. After both sides had won two Tests, huge attention focused on the decider at Melbourne and over 100,000 crowded into the ground during the five days to watch absorbing cricket and eventual English victory in the match and rubber.

The Golden Age of Cricket

CRICKET MATCH BETWEEN THE Australian Eleven AND THE EARL OF SHEFFIELD'S ELEVEN Sheffield Park — May 12th 1896

2d. — Sheffield Park — **Cricket Ground** — **2d.**

MONDAY, TUESDAY and WEDNESDAY, May 11, 12, 13, 1896,

Lord Sheffield's XI. v. Australians.

AUSTRALIANS.	First Innings		Second Innings	
Mr. H. Donnan	b Fry	32	c Hearne b Davidson	25
Mr. J. Darling	c Lilley b Mold	67	c Ranjitsinhji b Hearne	35
Mr. G. Giffen	c Lilley b Jackson	38	b Mold	18
Mr. F. A. Iredale	b Grace	14	c Lilley b Davidson	11
Mr. G. H. S. Trott (cap.)	c Ranjitsinhji b Hearne	43	not out	59
Mr. S. E. Gregory	b Grace	6	run out	0
Mr. C. Hill	c Lilley b Mold	32	b Davidson	23
Mr. C. J. Eady	c Hearne b Mold	2	c Lilley b Pougher	19
Mr. J. J. Kelly	not out	2	b Hearne	9
Mr. E. Jones	b Mold	9	c Ranjitsinhji b Pougher	0
Mr. T. R. McKibbin	st Lilley b Hearne	0	b Pougher	4
	b 10 l-b 1 w 1 n-b. Total	12	b, l.-b. w. n.-b. Total	
	Total — 257		**Total — 194**	

1-92 2-110 3-145 4-175 5-192 6-242 7-243 8-245 9-256 10-257
1-52 2-68 3-87 4-89 5-126 6-168 7-168 8-186 9-186 10-194

LORD SHEFFIELD'S XI.	First Innings		Second Innings	
1 Mr. W. G. Grace (capt.)	c Kelly b Jones	49	c Giffen b Jones	26
2 Mr. F. S. Jackson	c Hill b Jones	17	not out	95
6 Shrewsbury	c Donnan b Jones	1		
3 Gunn	c Giffen b Jones	5	c Hill b Eady	6
4 K. S. Ranjitsinhji	c Iredale b Jones	79	c Donnan b Jones	42
5 Mr. C. B. Fry	b Jones	4	b Trott	5
7 A. Hearne	c Kelly b Eady	4		
8 Lilley	c and b McKibbin	21		
10 Davidson	b Jones	4		
9 Pougher	not out	10		
11 Mold	run out	0		
	b 2 l-b 1 w 2 n-b. Total	5	b 4 l-b 1 w. n.-b. Total	6
	Total — 195		**Total — 180**	

1-58 2-60 3-71 4-80 5-80 6-110 7-166 8-183 9-186 10-195
1-45 2-86 3-176 4-180 5- 6- 7- 8- 9- 10-

Umpires—R. Thomas & W. A. J. West   Scorers—Ferg. A. Lemon & E. J. Taylor

Crowhurst, Printer to the S.C.C.C., 50-1-2 Market St., Brighton.

Lord Sheffield traditionally opened Australian tours to England with a game against his XI at his Sussex home. He always put both sides up at a hotel and once expressed disappointment at how little they had drunk.

It was the curtain-raiser on an era of England–Australia cricket which has few, if any, equals for excitement, popularity, quality of play and evenness of fortune. Both here and in Australia crowds poured in in thousands to watch the matches. The advantage swung back and forth from one country to the other; Stoddart's tour was the first of twelve series up to 1914 of which each side won six, three each at home and away. Only the last, in 1912, during the unsatisfactory Triangular Tournament including South Africa, when half of the leading Australian players had refused to tour after a row with their Board, was a disappointment. Discounting England's single win in this year, both sides won six matches in England while Australia enjoyed the advantage at home, winning 17 to England's 13. (The disparity in the totals in the two countries was partly the result of Tests in England being limited to three days, thereby increasing the possibility of a draw and, to a lesser extent, of weather preventing a result.)

The period saw the matches between England and Australia elevated to a position of unrivalled importance. Even during the early 1890s a number of county captains and committees viewed them as an unwelcome intrusion into the domestic season which only benefited a tiny minority of grounds and clubs. Few people would have compared the Tests to the annual fixtures between Gentlemen and Players for prestige and standards of play. But by 1914 there was no question that they were the most important and keenly awaited fixtures. With Test series expanded from three to five matches from 1899 and, from 1902, with a rota of six grounds – Headingley, Trent Bridge and Edgbaston being added to the original trio of Lord's, The Oval and Old Trafford – the impact of the matches grew accordingly. Lord Hawke was still preventing George Hirst and Wilfred Rhodes from joining Archie MacLaren's tour of 1901–02 and Schofield Haigh from being included for the Old Trafford Test of 1902 (when MacLaren was again captain) in the manner that he had refused to allow England's interests to supersede Yorkshire's for some years, but it was a rearguard action largely prompted by personal dislike of MacLaren and, as Test matches gained in importance, especially after the classic 1902 series, his lordship began to relent.

There is no question that, had the Australian sides of the period been weak, the matches would not have enjoyed such elevation in their status and popularity. Far from this being the case, for the four series of 1896, 1899, 1902 and 1905 they were strong in every department and, equally important, led by outstanding captains. Harry Trott on the first, and Joe Darling on the subsequent three tours, were two of the shrewdest and firmest captains in Australia's history and the importance of their leadership is best illustrated by comparison with the unhappy and unsuccessful visits of 1893 and 1912, led by Jack Blackham and Syd Gregory respectively, neither of whom were either tacticians or figures of authority.

The 1912 tour was summed up by Jack Pollard in *The Turbulent Years of Australian Cricket, 1893–1917*.

> The Australians who went to England for the 1912 Triangular Tournament were not only a poor cricket team but misbehaved so consistently they were socially ostracised long before the tour ended. They had an abysmal record in one of the wettest summers England had known and as the failures multiplied or they were forced to spend another day watching the rain tumble down they took solace in the bar. Part of the trouble was that their captain Syd Gregory was too kind-hearted and refused to impose any kind of discipline. He had no gift for command and could not see through the loafers and malingerers.

It was a far cry from the triumphs of a decade earlier when, in an equally wet summer, Joe Darling's 1902 side raised the levels of Anglo–Australian competition to new heights. Darling, a non-smoking, teetotal Presbyterian, would not have tolerated 'loafers and malingerers' even if he had had any in his side. He was forced to show great tenacity in pursuing his cricket career, for his wealthy wheat-farming family thoroughly disapproved of his interest in the game and constantly attempted to force him to devote himself to their properties. During the 1901–02 tour by England they were successful to the extent of persuading him to give up his captaincy of Australia and return to the farms in Tasmania after the Third Test. In England he ran his tours in the best traditions of a sergeant-major, constant authority tempered with fairness and the occasional gesture of reassuring generosity. If he showed little generosity towards his opponents, and was easily roused – as when the groundsman at Bramall Lane illegally watered the pitch

Joe Darling in 1899.

before the last day and, although Australia won, Darling refused to give him the traditional tip – he rarely displayed the abrasiveness of, say, Warwick Armstrong during the latter's period as Australia's captain.

Discipline imposed by captaincy reflected a greater element of control in the Australians' play, which contributed to the improvement of their fortunes. Previously their sides had always contained a couple of batsmen who would probably score runs in a vigorous and entertaining fashion and one or two bowlers who would take wickets. But all too often shortage of all-round depth and a lack of reliability – batsmen who could defend and bowlers who could tie batsmen down – proved their downfall. The degree to which this had changed was first demonstrated in England on the 1896 tour and thereafter with increasing forcefulness.

In addition to their ability, the attraction of the Australian cricketers was increased by their personalities. While the attitude of some Englishmen was little short of condescending, the huge majority of the sporting fraternity and English crowds greatly enjoyed the Australians' forthright lack of humbug and their vitality. To a society as insular as Edwardian England they were a source of considerable fascination comparable to, if not quite so extreme, the interest in Ranjitsinhji's Indian origins. They played as amateurs to fit in with English convention, but otherwise social niceties were of little importance and in many cases the amateur label was something of an anomaly.

One player who would hardly have qualified as a gentleman was the fast bowler Ernest Jones, a powerful ex-miner from South Australia. During the Australians' first match of the 1896 tour, against Lord Sheffield's XI at his lordship's Sussex home, 'Jonah' was introduced to the Prince of Wales who was a spectator. On hearing of Jonah's South Australian origins, the prince asked politely whether he attended St Peter's College, Adelaide. He must have been completely taken aback by Jonah's reply, 'Yes sir, I take the dust-cart there regularly.' During the 1899 tour, if Jones was not playing in any of the games immediately prior to a Test, Darling made sure that he was twelfth man, thereby ensuring that he was kept on the ground and unable to disappear for a potentially disastrous drinking session.

Despite popular misconceptions the Australians were by no means all rough diamonds. There was one player who dispelled such theories and, at the same time, ensured that attitudes to Australian cricketers would forever after be influenced by respect and affection: Victor Trumper. Trumper first toured England in 1899 aged 21 and died of Bright's disease in 1915, aged only 37. His premature death added to the lustre of his career, but far more important was his modest, unspoilt courtesy – the antithesis of the popularly conceived big and brash Australian. The names of only two or three other cricketers in history inspire a sense of such romantic nostalgia as Victor Trumper's, and his contribution to the image of Australian cricketers was immeasurable.

Trumper was too young to be considered for the 1896 tour to England but Clem Hill, who was only a few months older than Trumper, had proved himself sufficiently to be included in the party. Aged 16, Hill had scored 360 in an inter-college match. Against Stoddart's team in 1895 he scored 150 and 56 for South Australia when still only 18, but his selection was clinched by scoring 206 for South Australia against a New South Wales side that included one of the selectors. Hill was to become second only to Trumper as the most charismatic Australian batsman of the Edwardian era, but quite different in temperament and style. A strongly built left-hander, he crouched at the wicket almost in the manner of Jessop and ruthlessly attacked anything but the best bowling.

Clem Hill failed in all three Tests of the 1896 tour, making double figures only once in six innings, but his batting was an important factor in the Australians being unbeaten in all their county matches. He was one of seven batsmen who scored over 1,000 runs on the tour and between them made 18 hundreds. With Hill the other six – Iredale, Darling, Giffin, Trott, Gregory and Donnan – demonstrated the depth and variety the Australian side had assembled. Joe Darling, also on his first tour, was, like Hill, a first-class left-hander. When H.S. Altham produced *A History of Cricket* in 1926 he wrote that they were, 'by far the most formidable pair of left-handers that ever appeared together on the same [Test] side', and it is difficult to think of a pair that have superseded them since. The most attractive batsman was Frank Iredale, who opened with Darling.

The bowlers were equally effective. Jones's pace and aggression astonished onlookers and alarmed most batsmen who had to face him. Although there were a number of suggestions that he threw – as were made about his partner McKibbin who headed the Australian tour averages – no one took any action. It was in the match against Lord Sheffield's XI which launched the tour that Jones bowled the famous ball through W.G. Grace's beard, but more significant was the fact that neither Arthur Shrewsbury

*Clem Hill, whose attacking left-handed batting so often gave his team a decisive
start and whose name is most often linked with that of Trumper.*

nor his Nottinghamshire partner William Gunn fancied facing Jones in this match and both deliberately gave their wickets away. The major bowling contribution came from the medium-paced all-rounder Hugh Trumble, a hugely tall man with an unforgettably lugubrious face who toured England five times between 1890 and 1902 and once described bowling in Australia as 'a black man's job'. He was a masterly tactician who took his wickets with a combination of skill and cunning.

In the Second Test at Old Trafford the Australians got over the disappointment of the First at Lord's – when they were bowled out for 53 in their first innings and England went on to an easy victory despite a partnership of 221 by Trott and Gregory – and came back to win a thrilling match. The two outstanding individual performances at Old Trafford were by Ranjitsinhji who scored 62 and 154 not out in his first Test and Richardson who bowled 110 overs and took 13 wickets. Needing 125 in the last innings, Australia struggled towards victory, but when the England wicket-keeper Lilley dropped Kelly when 25 were needed it was, as *The Times* said afterwards, 'an irreparable blunder' and Australia got home by three wickets. With the series level, the last match at The Oval was keenly anticipated. A flurry of sensation was caused before a ball was even bowled by the strike of five English professionals – Abel, Hayward, Richardson, Lohmann and Gunn. Once this had blown over it was a bowler's match due to heavy rain and, needing 111 in the last innings, Australia could only manage 44. For England Peel and Hearne took 18 wickets between them and for Australia Trumble took six in each England innings.

Nobody questioned that the Australians had proved themselves on the tour and many considered that they were unlucky to have lost the Test rubber. All the same, when A.E. Stoddart set off in the winter of 1897–98 on his second tour with another formidable side among whom Ranji was the main attraction, English confidence was understandably high. It seemed to be justified, with victory by nine wickets in the First Test, Ranji scoring 175 in his first Test in Australia. Thereafter the situation changed dramatically and Australia won the remaining four Tests to recapture the Ashes for only the second time in the last 12 series.

Darling and Hill came into their own as Test batsmen, the former with three hundreds in the Tests and Hill with 188 in the Fourth Test, but for some of the English players their main opposition seemed to come primarily from some of the spectators who treated the visitors to humorous and occasionally offensive barracking. After the Third Test at Adelaide Ranji was reported to say that he would never play there again. Although the good-humoured prince soon got over his anger, Stoddart weighed in at a farewell banquet.

I have a right as an English cricketer who has been out here so often to make reference to the insults that have poured upon me and my team during our journey through Australia. We have been treated more like prize-fighters than a group of sportsmen and incurred the wrath of spectators and the Press in a manner that is totally undeserved.

Most Australians decided that Stoddart was happy to put up with a bit of good-humoured

*The Oval 1896: appreciation by the crowd after England had won the game
and the first of four memorable series.*

abuse when he was winning but took exception when fortune went the other way – an early example of the 'whingeing Pom'.

Having won the Ashes Australia were destined to retain them for the next three series, something that neither country achieved again until the 1960s. In 1899 Joe Darling led a team which, especially in its batting, was the strongest ever to leave Australia, which was just as well as they would be up against the youthful cream of England's Edwardian best. The most significant decision for Australia's future was made at the eleventh hour before the ship sailed. Originally the three selectors – Trumble, Darling and Syd Gregory – had decided against including Victor Trumper on the grounds that he was too young, despite Trumper's obviously prodigious talent. In the final match before the departure, however, when the Australian side were playing the last of three traditional games against 'the Rest' at Adelaide, the first two having been at Sydney and Melbourne, Trumper scored 75 in such style that the selectors were won over and the callow youth became the fourteenth member of the party, on a lower financial rate than the others and on the understanding that he helped the manager with such chores as dealing with autograph-hunters and the team's laundry.

In one sense 1899 marked full recognition of Australian tours, for the Test series was extended to five matches. The first, at Nottingham, was a watershed in English cricket: for W.G. Grace, aged 50, it was his last Test; for Wilfred Rhodes, aged 21, it was the first of a career that was to see him become the only cricketer to play in Tests at a greater age than Grace. Rhodes took seven wickets, but for the Old Man the ground was too far away and he knew that it was all over. 'That's it, Jacker, I shall never play again,' he said despondently to Stanley Jackson after the game. The Australians had the best of a draw but were irked by suspicion that they were deprived of victory by the blatantly partisan umpiring of R.G. Barlow (of Francis Thompson's 'O my Hornby and my Barlow long ago' fame) who gave Ranjitsinhji not out early in his match-saving innings of 93 in England's second innings.

The Second Test at Lord's decided the series in emphatic style for the Australians who won by ten wickets. Thereafter the subsequent three games were all drawn – the Third as a result of rain and the last two when Australia grimly held on to their one-match lead in the face of large England scores. The Lord's game was won by Australia's two young star batsmen, Hill and Trumper, both of whom scored 135, Trumper carrying his bat. This was Trumper's one major innings during the Test matches but his batting

Victor Trumper on the attack; perhaps the most
famous cricket photograph.

throughout the tour was a revelation. It is difficult to imagine the impact he had, not only for his batting but also his appearance and personality. They were accustomed to an altogether more brawny kind of Australian, with a thick moustache, rather than this delicate young man who, other than his habitual scruffy untidiness, had all the looks of a former English public schoolboy.

Trumper scored a total of 1,556 runs on the tour and the high spot came at Hove when, after Sussex had scored 414, Trumper led an Australian reply of 624 with 300 not out, the highest score by an Australian in England. Afterwards Darling asked his team to agree to Trumper being promoted to the same financial status as the rest of them. As Jack Pollard described, Trumper thanked him with characteristic modesty. 'Weeks later Darling was rummaging in his cricket bag when he found the bat with which Trumper had made the record score. On it Trumper had written, "To Joe Darling with V. Trumper's compliments." ' No wonder Frank Iredale once said of Trumper, 'To be near him always seemed to me to be an honour . . . I never knew a man who practised self-effacement as much as he.'

There was an enjoyable Australian footnote to the year, provided by one of their expatriates, Albert Trott, against his visiting compatriots. Trott had been one of the leading lights of the Australian side against Stoddart's 1894–95 tourists but, to general amazement, was left out of the 1896 side to England. He decided to journey to England where he took up a contract with Middlesex at Lord's. Playing for MCC and Ground he made history in 1899, when he followed two enormous sixes into the Lord's pavilion off Trumble by hitting Monty Noble clean over the pavilion, the only time such a hit has been made.

In the winter of 1901–02 the MCC had declined an invitation from the Australians once they discovered that many of the leading players – Ranjitsinhji, Jackson and Fry, to name three – would not be available. The invitation was passed to Archie MacLaren who, never one to admit the impossible, took out what was destined to be the last privately organized tour. The gaps left by those unavailable – to whose list had been added the names of Hirst and Rhodes – were filled by a number of new faces, in particular S.F. Barnes who was MacLaren's discovery. All went well in the First Test when MacLaren himself scored a hundred, Barnes took six wickets and England won by the decisive margin of an innings and 124 runs. But the future shape of things was clearly mapped out in the Second Test when, despite Barnes taking 11 wickets, Australia won by 229 runs. Injury prevented Barnes taking any further part in the Tests and the pattern of 1897–98 was repeated, Australia winning the three remaining Tests.

Australia's batsmen produced a number of fine innings, notably Hill who made successive scores of 99, 98 and 97, but the match-winning performances were the bowling of Trumble and Monty Noble. In the Second Test they took all 20 English wickets, in the Third it was 12, in the Fourth 11 and in the Fifth 15. In their different ways they were representative of the sort of cricketers Australia was producing by the turn of the century: gifted, competitive and thinking all-rounders who, at the same time as being able to win a game with either bat or ball, could also do so with their judgement.

Joe Darling led his second tour to England in 1902, assured of the strength and talent of his own side but with no illusions about the formidable potential of his opponents.

Darling's 1902 side, considered to be the strongest to leave Australia.
Standing: E. Jones, H. Trumble, Major Wardill, W.W. Armstrong, A.J. Hopkins,
R.A. Duff; seated: V.T. Trumper, M.A. Noble, J. Darling, J.V. Saunders,
J.J. Kelly; front: H. Carter, S.E. Gregory. Clem Hill is missing.

Despite depressingly bad weather throughout the summer, the Test series developed into a classic and the various matches have been as revived in subsequent writing as often as any others. The first two were both spoilt by rain and drawn; in the First England's batting line-up, which consisted of 11 players who were all first-class century-makers, might not have lived up to all expectations without 138 from J.T. Tyldesley, while the rain saved Australia who were bowled out in their first innings for 36. In the Second there was just over an hour and a half's play. The Third Test was the only one ever played at Sheffield's gloomy Bramall Lane ground and Australia asserted themselves with a victory by 143 runs.

It was the last two games which established the series in the top flight of Test cricket. Both had close finishes and honours were shared: Australia won at Old Trafford by three runs and England came back to win at The Oval by one wicket. The Old Trafford Test was ushered in by a series of decisions by the England selectors which caused little short of a furore and had a crucial impact on the outcome. Somerset's elegant opening batsman Lionel Palairet was picked instead of Gilbert Jessop, who would have been favoured by the England captain, MacLaren, who was not among the selectors, Stanley Jackson and A.C. Steel being co-opted to join the regular trio of Lord Hawke, Gregor MacGregor and H.W. Bainbridge. S.F. Barnes, who had a suspected injury, was dropped for

Lockwood, but the main bone of contention was raised over the inclusion of the luckless Fred Tate of Sussex. The selectors decided that, given the likelihood of rain, they needed an established wet-wicket bowler and opted for Yorkshire's Schofield Haigh. Lord Hawke, however, who was already facing up to losing Hirst, Rhodes and Jackson from his side, would have nothing of it and, refusing to release Haigh, put up Tate in his place. So incensed was Archie MacLaren that on the first morning of the match he deliberately left out George Hirst to idle away the three days as twelfth man. It was a quid pro quo born out of sheer personal antagonism.

In the end Victor Trumper virtually settled the matter single-handed. In response to his captain's request for a quick start, he became the first man to make a hundred before lunch on the first day. After heavy rain the night before, the wicket was dead but becoming increasingly sticky. After the strong start of Trumper, his opening partner R.A. Duff, and Clem Hill, the only Australian to make double figures was the redoubtable Darling with 51. In reply England managed to survive until the end of the day and on the second were taken to within 37 runs of the Australian total by Jackson who scored 138 and Len Braund of Somerset with 65.

In reply Australia were heading for disaster at 16 for three when Fred Tate made his unfortunate entry. He was moved by MacLaren to deep long leg, after the bowler Braund had requested that his Somerset compatriot Palairet was moved in to his customary position at short leg. Unlike Palairet, Tate was not renowned for his catching, and when almost immediately Darling skied a catch to him he dropped it. Darling went on to make 37 priceless runs, the highest score in Australia's total of 86.

Needing 123 to win England struggled towards the elusive target until eventually Fred Tate came in at number eleven with eight runs needed. Before he had faced a ball the players were driven back into the pavilion by rain. After three-quarters of an hour, play was resumed and Tate edged half the runs with a four. There his scrap of luck began and ended: three balls later he was bowled and Australia had won by three runs. Describing the match many years afterwards Cardus wrote, 'Fred Tate was made for pastoral humours at Horsham, not for thunder against the Gods on Olympus.' Tate himself never got over the match and his gloomy prediction to Len Braund afterwards that 'it'll never be forgotten' was sadly correct. It was his one and only appearance for England.

Similarly epic events were enacted a few weeks later at The Oval, with the weather again affecting but not ending the game. After Australia had scored 324 England only just avoided following-on but, largely thanks to the bowling of Lockwood who took five for 45, managed to restrict Australia to 121 in their second innings. Nonetheless the 263 runs required for victory seemed a hopelessly tall order on a wicket which had been deluged by overnight rain before the last day and was drying out to become increasingly receptive to spin. Pessimism was borne out with the score at 48 for five, and even the sight of Jessop striding to the wicket offered little cause for enthusiasm. Seventy-five minutes later Jessop had completed the most remarkable piece of hitting in Test history when he was caught by Noble at backward square leg for 104.

According to the playwright Ben Travers who was amongst the spectators, 'Jessop went absolutely crazy' and when he reached his hundred the crowd erupted as bowlers and boaters were flung into the air, most never to be retrieved despite probably costing

The England side for the first two Tests of the 1902 series. Standing:
G.H. Hirst, A.A. Lilley, W.H. Lockwood, L.C. Braund, W. Rhodes; seated:
C.B. Fry, F.S. Jackson, A.C. MacLaren, K.S. Ranjitsinhji, G.L. Jessop,
J.T. Tyldesley (on arm of seat).

three shillings. With Jackson, who made 49, Jessop took the score from 48 to 157, and after Jessop's departure George Hirst pushed remorselessly on, eventually to be not out on 58. With 15 runs needed he was joined by his fellow Yorkshireman Rhodes, and together they enacted the last-wicket partnership that took England to victory.

The last two Tests produced nerve-jangling excitement, with a number of heroes, but taking Australia's tour as a whole the batting of Victor Trumper shone out. It was primarily responsible for the pre-eminent reputation that posterity has afforded him — certainly as far as English observers were concerned. On often abominable wickets he scored 2,578 runs, but never more than 128; after making a hundred he preferred to let someone else have a go. He habitually batted in a thick turtle-necked jumper, and throughout the tour Darling was concerned that Trumper's health might give way. Any frailty was banished when Trumper was at the wicket and bowling was dealt with in the manner described by Cardus, recalling Archie MacLaren defending himself against humorous suggestions that he had failed to contain Trumper during his hundred before lunch at Old Trafford.

MacLaren, who adored an argument, rose to the bait; he took lumps of sugar out of the basin and set them all over the table, saying 'Gaps be damned! Good God I know my man — Victor had half a dozen strokes for the same kind of ball. I exploited the inner and outer ring — a man there, a man there and another man covering him.' (He banged

Surrey County Cricket Club.

KENNINGTON OVAL, AUGUST, 11, 12 & 13, 1902

ENGLAND v. AUSTRALIA.

AUSTRALIA.	First Innings		Second Innings	
1 Mr. V. Trumper ...	... b Hirst...	42	run out	2
2 Mr. R. A. Duff	... c Lilley, b Hirst ...	23	b Lockwood	6
3 Mr. C. Hill	... b Hirst...	11	c MacLaren, b Hirst ...	34
4 Mr. J. Darling	... c Lilley, b Hirst	3	c MacLaren, b Lockwood	15
5 Mr. M. A. Noble ...	... c & b Jackson	52	b Braund	13
6 Mr. S. E. Gregory ...	... b Hirst	23	b Braund	9
7 Mr. W W. Armstrong	... b Jackson	17	b Lockwood	21
8 Mr. A. Hopkins ...	... c MacLaren, b Lockwood	40	c Lilley, b Lockwood ...	3
9 Mr. H. Trumble ...	... not out	64	not out	7
10 Mr. J. Kelly	... c Rhodes, b Braund ...	39	l-b-w, b Lockwood ...	0
11 Mr. J. V. Saunders ...	... l-b-w, b Braund	0	c Tyldesley, b Rhodes ...	2
	B 5, l-b 3, w , n-b 2 ..	10	B 7, l-b 2, w , n-b , ...	9
	Total ...	324	Total ...	121

1st Innings ... 1 for 47   2-63   3-69   4-82   5-126   6-174   7-175   8-256   9-324

2nd Innings   1 for 6   2-9   3-31   4-71   5-75   6-91   7-99   8-114   9-115

ENGLAND.	First Innings.		Second Innings.	
1 Mr. A. C. MacLaren	... c Armstrong, b Trumble	10	b Saunders	2
2 Mr. L. C. H. Palairet	... b Trumole	20	b Saunders	6
3 Tyldesley	... b Trumble	33	b Saunders	0
4 Hayward ..	... b Trumble	0	c Kelly, b Saunders ...	7
5 Hon. F. S. Jackson ...	... c Armstrong, b Saunders	2	c & b Trumble ...	49
6 Braund ...	.. c Hill, b Trumble ...	22	c Kelly b Trumble ...	2
7 Mr. G. L. Jessop ...	... b Trumble	13	c Noble, b Armstrong	104
8 Hirst	.. c & b Trumble	43	not out |... ...	58
9 Lockwood	... c Noble, b Saunders ...	25	l-b-w, Trumble	2
10 Lilley	... c Trumper, b Trumble ...	0	c Darling, b Trumble ...	16
11 Rhodes	not out	0	not out	6
	B 13, l-b 2, w , n-b , ...	15	B 5 l-b 6, w , n-b , ...	11
	Total ...	183	Total	263

1st Innings ... 1 for 31   2-36   3-62   4 67   5-67   6-83   7-137   8-179   9-183

2nd Innings   1 for 5   2-5   3-10   4-31   5-48   6-157   7-187   8-214   9 248

Price 1d.

Printed on the Ground by Merritt & Hatcher, Ltd.
168, Upper Thames Street, E.C.

Umpires—Richardson & A. A. White.   Stumps drawn 6.30 p.m.

RESULT.—ENGLAND WON BY ONE WICKET.

The scorecard of the 1902 Oval Test, one of the most dramatic in history.

the lumps of sugar down one by one, punctuating his luminous discourse.) 'I told my bowlers to pitch on the short side to the off: I set my heart and brain on every detail of our policy. Well, in the third over of the morning Victor hit two balls straight into the practice ground, high over the screen behind the bowler. I couldn't very well have had a man fielding in the bloody practice ground, now could I?

Archie MacLaren's differences with Lord Hawke came to a head when the 1903–04 tour to Australia was being arranged. As expected, the MCC had agreed to take responsibility for the tour, and first approached Stanley Jackson as to his availability to go as captain. Jackson declined and the position was offered to P.F. Warner of Middlesex, aged 29, who had occasionally captained his county but had never played for England. He had, however, been a member of Lord Hawke's tours to the West Indies in 1896–97, to South Africa in 1898–99 and to Australia in 1902–03. MacLaren's considerable pride was severely dented and he refused to join the tour. Despite the fact that he had lost three successive series, in his eyes he was the established captain of England and he had been deliberately passed over.

In the event, the MCC's decision was a huge success and, at a time when many felt that English honour was at stake after the loss of four successive series, Warner's team

Warner's 1903–04 tour to Australia was the first under MCC auspices and achieved a notable success in regaining the Ashes.

successfully regained the Ashes by winning the series 3–2. Warner himself, completely devoted to cricket, immersed himself in the business of captaincy on and off the field, and his enthusiasm and determination provided impressive leadership. It was his decision that, for the first time on a tour to Australia, the amateurs and professionals stayed at the same hotels. Off the field Warner set great store by social behaviour as commented on many years afterwards by George Lyttelton, for whom there was always something a little priggish about 'Plum'. Lyttelton wrote caustically that Warner filled his tour accounts with:

> . . . stuff like 'I shall never forget the wonderful hospitality of the Governor of New South Wales and his gracious lady,' which one could write without going nearer to N.S.W. than the lavatory at Victoria, when what would be of passing Pepysian interest is to hear what Darling said to Trumper when he had a devilled cold pork-chop for breakfast on the morning of a Test Match.

Warner's team contained seven faces new to Australia, three of whom in particular, R.E. Foster, Wilfred Rhodes and B.J.T. Bosanquet, made crucial contributions. In the First Test Foster made 287 in England's first innings, which remains easily the highest score made by any batsman in his first Test. In Australia's second innings Trumper played what many people considered the most brilliant innings of his career to score 185, but England were able to win by five wickets. In the Second Rhodes took a record 15 for 124 and England won by 185 runs. In all Rhodes took 31 wickets in the five Tests. After Australia had won the Third Test, the Fourth at Sydney was played on a rain-affected wicket, and when Australia were chasing 329 in their second innings Warner produced Bosanquet who, bewildering the batsmen with his googly, at one stage had taken five wickets for 12 runs and ended with six for 51 to give England the victory which secured the rubber.

Australia asserted themselves with a convincing win in the final Test, and it was fitting that the victory was largely brought about by the bowling of Hugh Trumble in his last Test match. He had bowed out of England after five visits by taking 12 wickets in the Oval Test of 1902, and now he took seven for 28, including a hat-trick, in England's second innings. Trumble was Australia's greatest bowler of the Edwardian era, who never allowed his serious approach to cricket to disguise his native Australian humour. His presence on the cricket field was well described by C.B. Fry.

> I would prefer not to see Hughie Trumble against me in flannels, for the simple reason that he is the most long-headed, observant and acute judge of the game, a perfect master of the whole art of placing fieldsmen and changing bowlers. It is his head – that long, solemn head, I should fear if I were England's captain, not his bowling arm or spinning fingers, deft as they are. It is the head, the best of the side, that made Hugh Trumble the big difference to the Australians.

There is no doubt that the Australians felt the loss of Trumble keenly when they visited England in 1905 for what became known as 'Jackson's year'. Not surprisingly.

*Warwick Armstrong, a formidable Australian in every sense, coming out to bat
in 1909.*

Captaining England for the first time in what was to be his last series, he won all five
tosses, headed the English batting and bowling averages and won the rubber 2–0. Despite
never having captained Yorkshire, his strategy and judgement were on a par with the
experienced Joe Darling who was leading his third and final tour. England's batting
strength was formidable and the most sparkling play came from MacLaren, Tyldesley and
Jackson himself, as well as Fry, on account of his 144 in the last Test at The Oval. In their
two victories they managed to capitalize upon strong individual innings in a manner that
Australia were never able to do. Trumper, injured in the First Test and thereafter
troubled by ill-health, did not show his form of 1902. For once his opening partner Duff
was not eclipsed and he matched Fry's batting at The Oval by scoring 146 in what proved
to be his last Test. Taking the tour as a whole, the most impressive member of the team,
not least for his enormous size and uncompromising personality, was Warwick
Armstrong, who scored nearly 2,000 runs, including 303 not out against Somerset, and
took 122 wickets but, like most of the team, he was not at his best in the Tests.

For a number of reasons the 1905 series marked the end of an era. By the time England
next visited Australia, in the winter of 1907–08, the tour had already been delayed by
one year thanks to the mushrooming row in Australia over the establishment of a Board
of Control. Both the old-established authorities in Sydney, Melbourne and Adelaide –
who also vied with each other – and the players, all of whose influence was threatened,
vigorously opposed the move and the struggle dominated Australian cricket until 1914.
Despite the usual amateur absentees, many of the best-known English faces were missing
in the far-from-representative team. The tour was led by the Nottinghamshire captain
A.O. Jones, but illness prevented him from playing in any of the first three Tests when

F.L. Fane, the second senior amateur whose previous Test experience had been in South Africa in 1905–06, took over.

For Australia Monty Noble had taken over from Joe Darling and was soon to prove himself in the same class as a captain. His leadership was a major factor in Australia's emphatic 4–1 win in the series, for while his established batsmen all played at least one decisive innings – Hill made 87 in the First Test and 160 in the Third, Armstrong 133 not out in the Fourth, while best of all was Trumper's 166 in the final Test – there were impressive displays by some of the new England faces. George Gunn, in Australia for his health and called up at the last minute to replace Jones, scored 119 and 74 in the First Test (his first) and 122 not out in the last, K.L. Hutchings scored 126 in his second, and Jack Hobbs, brought into the side for the Second Test, marked his début with 83 and by the end of the tour was – quite rightly – universally regarded by Australians as the rising star among young England professionals.

Monty Noble's leadership of the 1909 tour to England stamped him as one of the most powerful and effective captains in Test cricket. With nine of his players visiting England for the first time, he retained the Ashes with a 2–1 victory. Without Hill, who had declined to tour due to differences with the Australian Board, and Darling, who had retired, Noble's side was largely inexperienced and lacked the proven quality of the previous three sides, but he moulded them into a winning combination with two novices, Ransford and Bardsley – who became the first man to score a hundred in both innings of a Test at The Oval – outstanding among the batsmen. Strictness – in the field bowlers were regularly ordered to their wickets as the batsmen were running, and no drinking was allowed during Test matches – was balanced with encouragement, while his mind was constantly analysing the game and his next move. Most English observers maintained that he had no equal among his Australian contemporaries. Philip Trevor, writing in 1921, would have had him as captain of an imaginary Australian side from all periods. Charlie Macartney, a member of the 1909 side, was later glowing in his praise in his memoirs *My Cricketing Days*, describing Noble as 'a strong character, hard but just. His judgement of other players' capabilities was astonishing. Above all, he knew himself. Few captains of the all-round class bowled themselves neither too much nor too little as did Noble. He was a rare personality, and I know of none greater.'

Archie MacLaren was brought back to lead England, but it was not a happy series for him. Out of form with the bat, he won the First Test when, in a low-scoring match, Hirst and Blythe took all 20 Australian wickets, but he was soon at odds with the selectors – who tried 25 players during the five Tests – especially over the team for the Second Test at Lord's which Australia won emphatically by nine wickets. After this match MacLaren offered to give up the captaincy but Lord Hawke, for once his supporter, persuaded him to stay on, although with little joy. Australia won the Third Test by 126 runs, largely as a result of England's batting failure and the last two Tests were drawn. It was MacLaren's last Test and he could have been forgiven for pondering the ill-fortune which had dogged his captaincy of England and to an extent eclipsed his formidable tactical ability, especially as Monty Noble won all five tosses.

The 1909 series was the fourth in succession that England had lost at home but, not least because of the selection argument, the 1909 failures were viewed in a far more pessimistic light than the previous defeats when the general consensus was that the matches had been well balanced, the play of the highest quality and honours, if not even, fairly distributed. Therefore it was in the hope of not only victory but also restoring the prestige of English cricket that a side left to tour Australia in the winter of 1911–12.

Both aspirations were realized, for after Australia had won the First Test the visitors never looked back, winning the remaining four. Although Plum Warner led the tour out, he only played in the first match after arrival, being taken ill, and J.W.H.T. Douglas took over and captained all five Tests. A better boxer than cricketer – he won an Olympic gold medal – he was quite impervious to the vocal efforts of Australian supporters and the nickname they gave him 'Johnny Won't Hit Today' and encouraged his players to be similarly unaffected. He left Australia with the grudging affection and respect of most people.

England's strong batting was led by Hobbs, who scored hundreds in three successive Tests: 126, 187 and 178, the last of which was made in a record-breaking opening stand of 323 with Wilfred Rhodes who made 179. But the great feature of the tour was the bowling partnership of Sydney Barnes and Frank Foster, the 22-year-old captain of Warwickshire. Bowling on plumb wickets throughout the tour, their medium pace was relentlessly accurate and testing and, opening the attack in all five Tests, they bowled the huge majority of England's overs with devastating effect. At the end Barnes had taken 34 wickets and Foster 32.

Youthful enthusiasm and energy no doubt sustained Foster, but the experienced and uncompromising professional Barnes had no illusions about either his value or the workload he was being asked to shoulder. Having inspected the 'shirt-front' wicket at Melbourne on the blazing hot day which opened the Second Test, he marched into the

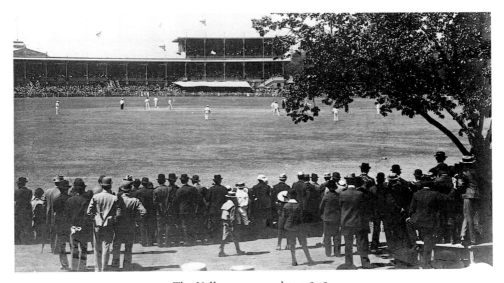

The Melbourne ground in 1898.

Some of the ill-fated 1912 Australian side arriving at Plymouth in the early morning.

pavilion and asked the England manager if he had seen the wicket. When the reply was negative Barnes retorted, 'Well I have . . . and I want half a bottle of wine.' Thus fortified he went out to dismiss the first four Australians in five overs while conceding only one run. At the end of just over an hour he had taken one more wicket and given away five more runs.

No doubt the behind-the-scenes machinations between the players and the Board of Control did not help Australia's cause. The bone of contention was who should appoint the manager of Australia's forthcoming visit to England in 1912, the players arguing that it was their long-established right, which was accepted in the Board's constitution, the Board arguing that the decision was theirs. Clem Hill, who was captaining Australia for the 1911–12 Tests, was a leading protagonist and actually came to blows with P.A. McAlister during the selection meeting for the Fourth Test. Frank Iredale, the third selector, was forced into the role of referee.

The issue came to a head in January 1912 when Hill headed a group of six of Australia's leading Test cricketers who wrote to the Board making it clear that if they could not choose their own player-manager they would not go to England for the proposed Triangular Tournament. The other five were Trumper, Armstrong, Ransford, Cotter and Carter. The Board made it clear that they would not give way and so the six did not go.

It was a sad end to the Test careers of two of Australia's outstanding batsmen from any period, Victor Trumper and Clem Hill, and it boded ill for Australia's chances in England. Thus the period ended on a low note for Australian cricket, but should be remembered for the glorious decade of 1899–1909.

8

OTHER VISITORS

The Edwardians revelled in the fierce competition provided by the Australians. At the same time they relished novelty, which was provided by the visitors during those summers in between the regular Australian tours, who added variety and their own distinctive flavour to the cricket of the period. In the case of the first two, the South Africans and West Indians, English imperialists could also enjoy the feeling that one of their cherished ways of life had been successfully exported and introduced to others. These were also to follow Australia as the next two countries to be given Test status. The third group, the Gentlemen of Philadelphia, were rather different; indeed they were a phenomenon of the period and as representative of the Edwardian spirit of amateurism as anything to be found in England. They blossomed on three visits to England in 1897, 1903 and 1908, when all their games were given first-class status. Thereafter cricket in Philadelphia wilted from its state of affluent good health, stifled by the war, the loss of leisure and the rise of baseball.

Cricket in South Africa had been well established in schools since the mid-nineteenth century, but it was a series of private tours from England during the 1880s and 1890s which gave the game vital impetus and launched South Africa towards Test status. Although all matches in South Africa from the English tour of 1888–89 are recorded as Tests, the most significant advance came in 1907 when for the first time the South Africans' games in England were given the status.

After the pioneering visits arranged by individuals, notably Lord Hawke who took two tours in 1895–96 and 1898–99, the breakthrough in the quality of South African cricket came in 1905–06 when the first official MCC side led by Plum Warner was decisively beaten 4–1. Warner's team may not have been a representative England side but there was no questioning its strength. In addition to the captain himself the main batsmen were the Yorkshire professional David Denton and the hard-hitting amateurs F.L. Fane and E.G. Wynyard. There were two all-rounders in the brilliant young amateur J.N. Crawford who had left school only a few months before the tour, and the Sussex professional A.E. Relf, while among the bowlers were Charlie Blythe of Kent and Schofield Haigh of Yorkshire.

The matting wickets of South Africa proved the downfall of a number of the batsmen – not least Warner himself – but the MCC side were outplayed both in batting and bowling, most significantly the latter. In the five Tests they only managed totals of over

THE PHILADELPHIAN CRICKETERS.

SOME SKETCHES OF THE PLAY AT THE OVAL MATCH
BY "RIP'S RIVAL."

A cartoonist's view of the Philadelphians who visited England in 1897.

200 runs twice whereas their opponents did so six times, including three totals of over 300. After the South African euphoria of their victory by one wicket in the First Test at Johannesburg, which Warner described as 'the best-fought match, everything considered, I have ever taken part in', their margins of victory were conclusive: nine wickets, 243 runs, and an innings and 16 runs. England's victory by four wickets in the Fourth Test was brought about by Blythe who took 11 for 118.

The most successful South African bowlers were the fast-medium S.J. Snooke and the medium-pace J.H. Sinclair who took 24 and 21 wickets respectively, but the series was memorable for the emergence of the googly-bowling quartet of Schwarz, White, Faulkner and Vogler. Schwarz had been born and educated in England and played occasional matches for Middlesex between 1901 and 1905. It was during those years that he learnt the googly from its 'inventor', B.J.T. Bosanquet, who was playing for Middlesex at the same time and who took Schwarz as a member of his 1901 tour of North America. Schwarz and White gave a taste of the googly-bowling combination during the South African visit to England in 1904, but their matches were not given Test status and the tour did not attract great attention.

Three years previously South Africa's first tour of the century was not helped by the fact that it took place at a time when the South African war against the Boers was in its worst year and had provoked not a little hostility as demonstrated by a letter to *The Times*.

> Sir, I observe that a team of cricketers is about to leave South Africa for this country. At a time like the present, with the call for young men to put an end to the deplorable state of affairs there, and when we ourselves are sending out the best of our manhood for that purpose, it is, to say the least of it, the most wretched taste for these young men to leave it on a cricket tour. I trust the British public will take this view of the matter. Next year we should be delighted to see them, but today it seems quite monstrous.

Despite these disadvantages, *Wisden*'s analysis of the visit leaves little doubt as to the editor's opinions.

> Though they obtained such a good proportion of victories it cannot be said that their presence in England meant much to the cricket public. Like other travelling teams in England they were not sufficiently near to the Australian standard to command attention and their matches entered into no sort of competition with county cricket.

By 1907 when, after the successes against Warner's side, the South African games in England were given Test status for the first time, the situation was very different and the editor was writing, 'So great was the interest excited by the matches that despite the bad weather the tour yielded a profit of, roughly speaking, £1400 – a striking and very pleasant contrast to the financial experience of previous trips.' Coverage of the tour was expanded enormously: it was moved out of the previous minor position after public schools cricket to first place in the coverage of the season's cricket – in front of the counties. Far more of an accolade were the selection of Schwarz and Vogler as two of the Five Cricketers of the Year, and the article among the features at the beginning contributed by R.E. Foster, the England captain who opposed the South Africans, entitled 'South African Bowling'.

Few people in England had an inkling of the cricketing coup which the South Africans would launch with their quartet of spinners in 1907. Even the members of the 1905–06

*The 1907 South Africans were the outstanding side of the country's first thirty
years of Test cricket. Standing: A.D. Nourse, H. Smith, W.A. Shalders,
M. Hathorn, G.A. Faulkner, G. Allsop (manager); seated: J.H. Sinclair,
R.O. Schwartz, Rev. C.W. Robinson, P.W. Sherwell, L.J. Tancred, A.E. Vogler,
J.J. Kotze; front: S.J. Snooke, G.C. White, S.D. Snooke.*

side felt that while the googly bowlers had mastered their native matting wickets, they
would not be so effective on the more varied and softer grass wickets in England,
especially in such a dismally wet summer as 1907 turned out to be from an early stage.
They were to be proved wrong, as the results of the tour confirm: of 27 first-class
matches the South Africans won 17 and only lost 4. In 1901 they had played 15, won 5
and lost 9. Sadly they failed to achieve their first Test win and, with nothing like as
formidable a side for many years afterwards, had to wait nearly thirty years to pass that
milestone. Their batting was not as powerful as at home on the matting wickets most of
the players had been brought up with, and at Leeds Charlie Blythe took 15 for 99 to give
England the one victory of the series, the other two matches being drawn.

With or without a Test win, the tour was a huge success and, as Warner wrote
afterwards, 'not since the days of the earlier Australian teams have any bowlers been
more talked about than Vogler, Schwarz, Faulkner and White. People used to flock to see
them bowl.' The most effective two were Schwarz, who by this time had almost
abandoned the googly for pure off-break bowling, and Vogler whom Foster described in
his *Wisden* article as being, 'in the writer's humble opinion the greatest bowler playing
cricket in either hemisphere at the present time'. His main skill was concealing the off-
break bowled with a leg-break action, which he and his henchmen had christened the
'wrong 'un'. He took 133 wickets on the tour. Schwarz, who took 143, ended with an

average of 11.79 which is the best among the élite group of five visiting bowlers whose average, for a total of more than 100 wickets, is lower than that of the leading home bowler. Nor did these two monopolize the acclaim. Both White and Faulkner took over 70 wickets and, after facing Faulkner in the Leeds Test, the England wicket-keeper concluded that 'it was like playing Briggs through the air and Richardson off the pitch'.

Almost the most significant aspect of the bowling was the effect that it had upon English batsmen, which Foster maintained to be enormous. He also had grave misgivings about the long-term effects upon the glories of batsmanship as practised by himself and his contemporaries, for he felt that, no longer feeling secure about making their shots – going for the cover drives and cuts – batsmen would be forced into nervous defence 'till those beautiful drives we are wont to expect from some of our greatest batsmen will become things of the past'. He cited the example of Tom Hayward, who was stumped in both the first two Tests going for a cover drive, arguing that Hayward would be far more cautious about trying the shot thereafter. To some extent Foster was proved right in that, during the last few seasons before the war, the flourishes of Edwardian batsmanship were disappearing, to go completely after 1919, and the new complexity of a spin attack was certainly a strong influence, if not the sole cause.

When England next visited South Africa, in the winter of 1909–10 with a team led by H.D.G. Leveson-Gower similar to the one led by Warner four years earlier, the googly bowlers maintained their superiority to enable South Africa to win the series 3–2. The main curiosity of the tour was that it witnessed the swansong of the underarm bowling of

Local colour for the members of the 1909–10 MCC tour to South Africa.

the nineteenth century. George Simpson-Hayward, an amateur who continued to play for Worcestershire until 1914, played in the only Test series of his career and, bowling his spinning underhand deliveries at a faster pace than the more customary 'lobs', was England's leading wicket-taker with 23 wickets, including six for 43 on his début in the first South African innings of the First Test. The matting wickets suited this secret weapon as well as they did the South Africans' own googlies.

Before England's tour of South Africa, in fact ever since the success of 1907, the main question on the Test agenda was the proposal for a Triangular Tournament put forward by the patron of South African cricket, Abe Bailey. A financier who had become hugely wealthy thanks to the gold and diamond riches of South Africa, Abe Bailey was unstinting in his support of South African tours and determined in his ambition for the country to be accepted on equal terms with England and Australia.

The fact that his proposal was accepted demonstrated the degree to which England was anxious to build up cordial relations with the whole of South Africa after the rift caused by the war, and the influence which magnates such as himself, born of the country's new-found wealth, had in English circles. Like the diamond-king brothers, Jack and Solly Joel, Abe Bailey was on friendly terms with Edward VII through his expansive career as a racehorse owner and, once accepted by the king, they were accepted elsewhere by all except the crustiest aristocrats. These entrepreneurs who had made their fortunes exploiting the wealth of the empire, before returning to England to enjoy the social advances which their money was able to bring, were an integral part of the Edwardian plutocracy.

In the end Abe Bailey's scheme was not the success he had envisaged. He had hoped to be able to replace the scheduled 1909 tour of England by Australia with his Triangular Tournament. At first his influence appeared to be winning the day and, despite the Australians' predictable lack of enthusiasm, the county representatives suggested that the MCC accept the scheme and the MCC informed the Australian Board of Control of the decision. In the end a letter from Stanley Jackson to *The Times* effectively quashed the scheme, such was his authority by this time, and the Australian tour went ahead as planned.

The Triangular Tournament was postponed until 1912, by which time England and Australia had both visited South Africa and South Africa had made their first trip to Australia in 1910–11. The Australian wickets offered little assistance to the spinners and, with Trumper showing a wonderful return to form, Australia won the Tests comfortably, 4–1. The feature of South Africa's play was the batting of Aubrey Faulkner, who scored over 700 runs in Tests and over 2,000 on the tour.

By 1912 Abe Bailey had become Sir Abe, but his South Africans were not the side they had been five years earlier. Vogler had retired and the magic had gone out of the other bowlers, while, of the batsmen, only Faulkner and the new discovery Herbie Taylor showed any sort of distinction. The tournament was a disaster for South Africa, who lost five out of their six matches and drew the other, and not much more of a success for the other two teams. The weather was dismal, the Australians were weakened by the lack of the six players who had stayed at home, while England were very strong. The partisan English crowds were only interested in turning up to matches in which England were

The three captains of the Triangular Tournament: Charles Fry between Frank Mitchell of South Africa (left) and Syd Gregory of Australia.

playing, especially once the South Africans had shown their weakness and they realized that the Australians were without most of the old favourites from past tours. Any plans for repeating the tournament in Australia and South Africa were abandoned and the only benefit from such a joint venture of imperial sportsmanship, which is how Sir Abe envisaged his idea, was the establishment in 1909 of the Imperial Cricket Conference which became the International Cricket Conference.

The 1900 West Indians, the first side to tour England. Standing: M.M. Kerr,
S.W. Sproston, G.L. Livingston, P.J. Cox, W.C. Nock, T.B. Burton,
L.S. D'Ade, C.A. Ollivierre; seated: W.S. Bowring, G.C. Learmond,
R.S.A. Warner, P.A. Goodman, L.S. Constantine; front: F.S. Hinds, S. Woods.

The colour distinction, which was subsequently to cause so much contention, unhappiness and the eventual expulsion of South Africa from the international cricket community, began during this first period of their international career. Although one coloured player, C.B. Llewellyn of Natal, did play in most series between 1904 and 1912, Rowland Bowen maintains in *Cricket: A History* that on the 1910–11 tour of Australia, 'He was tormented by his white fellow tourists to such an extent that for peace and quiet in the hotels where the team stayed he had to take refuge in the W.C.s and lock himself in.' Less speculative was the fact that South Africa's most formidable bowler of the 1890s, T. Hendricks, whom one member of Walter Read's side of 1890–91 described as 'the black Spofforth', was not chosen to play for his country because he was black.

No such discrimination occurred in the case of the two pioneering West Indian sides who visited England in 1900 and 1906. Both sides contained a balance of white West Indians of English origin and black West Indians which fitted into the Edwardian pattern in that it approximated to the amateur/professional division of English cricket. The main complication over choosing the side arose from the need to satisfy all the major cricketing islands, and as a result the team was chosen on a quota system which led to the omission of C.P. Cumberbatch of Trinidad, the most formidable West Indian bowler at the time. Trinidad were limited to four players: Aucher Warner (brother of Plum) who was the captain, L.S. Constantine (father of Learie), L.S. D'Ade and S. Woods, Cumberbatch's fast bowling partner. Barbados also supplied four players; British Guiana three including W.J. Burton, the other main bowler; Jamaica two; St Vincent one – C.A. Ollivierre, who proved to be the most successful batsman – and Grenada also one.

The teething problems that West Indian tours were to suffer were also shown by the fact that, while Burton and Woods played as professionals, the other black members of the side played as amateurs, the financial implications of which almost made their mark before the team sailed for England, as C.L.R. James described.

> The haphazard organization (and genuine enthusiasm) of West Indies cricket is shown by the experience of 'Old Cons' as he came to be called, even before his son became a famous cricketer. Selected to go, on the day the boat left he was seen standing disconsolately downtown. Asked if he was not going he replied no, he could not afford it. A public subscription was opened on the spot. A fast launch was chartered, the boat was caught before it left the Gulf of Paria and L.S. Constantine scrambled on board to hit the first West Indian century in England for West Indies v MCC at Lord's.

The matches of the 1900 tour were not given first-class status by the MCC and, although the visitors were overwhelmed by most of the county sides they met, there was no questioning the enjoyment and valuable experience of touring abroad and playing three-day matches. Sadly, heavy defeat by W.G. Grace's London County side at the Crystal Palace in the first match and in the opening county games dampened public enthusiasm and at most matches spectators were thin on the ground.

When the side travelled to Bristol to play Gloucestershire there were no doubt a few absent supporters who, when they heard the accounts of the match, wished they had bothered to turn up. After H. Wrathall and C.L. Townsend had both scored hundreds in a huge partnership, the Gloucestershire captain Gilbert Jessop strode to the wicket, no doubt with the intention of knocking off some quick runs. In the space of exactly an hour he put on 201 with Townsend – Jessop's share being 157 – in 60 minutes. Accounts of the match vary slightly but there is no doubt that Jessop's fantastic hitting was much enjoyed by the helpless West Indies bowlers and fielders, as the local paper reported:

> Nobody enjoyed this wonderful spell of phenomenal scoring more than the coloured men in the ranks of the visitors. The bowlers who were being punished, and the fielders who were called upon to work as they had probably never worked before, were hugely delighted. One of them would lie down and literally shake with laughter after a big hit, and the next minute would be making a futile effort to save another four from being placed to the credit of the batsman.

The rich comedy of the scene was rounded off when Woods, the main hope among the West Indies bowlers, approached his captain Warner and asked for permission to take off his boots and bowl at Jessop in bare feet, confident that returning to his accustomed state of comfort would do the trick. After his request was refused and Jessop had dispatched a few more balls over the ropes Woods tried again, this time limiting his request to one boot only, but Warner knew the importance of maintaining propriety and replied, 'Out of the question. You can't do that here.'

After the Gloucestershire débâcle Plum Warner joined the side to play against Leicestershire and, largely as a result of his opening partnership of 238 with Ollivierre, the West Indies secured victory by an innings and 87 runs. Thereafter they enjoyed mixed fortunes, but had the satisfaction of beating Hampshire and Surrey – the latter by the decisive margin of an innings and 34 runs. In all three victories the bowling of Woods and Burton, both of whom took over 70 wickets during the tour, was complemented by some high scores, notably by Ollivierre, who made 159 against Derbyshire and 94 against Surrey. In all he made 883 runs on the tour with Constantine next with 610.

The limited success enjoyed on this tour and the West Indies' showing against a strong side taken there by Lord Brackley in January 1905 persuaded the MCC to allow the matches of the 1906 tour to count as first-class. Expectations were not fulfilled, however, and in a programme including 13 first-class games – which *Wisden* considered to be far too ambitious – eight games were lost against three won. Once again heavy defeat in the first game against a side got up by W.G. Grace – his London County club having been disbanded by this time – damaged the tourists' chances of attracting favourable attention, and *Wisden* concluded that they 'failed to make any strong appeal to the public'. The almanack went on in slightly scathing tones, 'the players were not good enough to make the English counties feel in the smallest degree apprehensive'.

In the main this was probably a fair comment, but the Yorkshire batsmen who faced the visitors at Harrogate might not have agreed. The match was late in the tour, by which time the West Indians were beginning to find their form. Having scored 270 against a Yorkshire side which, if not representative, included Rhodes, Denton, Tunnicliffe and Taylor, they bowled out their hosts for 50, Richard Ollivierre taking seven for 23. Victory by 262 runs was the high spot of the tour. The best omen for the future came in the penultimate game, against Nottinghamshire, when the 18-year-old Barbadian George Challenor scored 108 against the county's regular opening attack of Wass and Hallam, in a manner which stamped him as a batsman with wonderful potential. Within a short time he had emerged as the West Indies' pre-eminent batsman, the only one who could claim a place among the stylists of the Edwardian era, and the founder of their tradition of exhilarating stroke-making.

The first team to have visited the West Indies came from the United States in 1887, and the best players in that side came from Philadelphia where cricket was played throughout the Edwardian era in surroundings of affluence and studied elegance only achieved in England at Lord's, the festivals and country houses. After recovery from the trauma of the Civil War, the development of a cricket-playing society was founded on the twin pillars of the city's commercial wealth and an unswerving code of amateurism exemplified by the club called Philadelphia Zingari, taking the name of England's élite I Zingari. The only professionals were erstwhile English players who were taken on as coaches and against whom an annual Gentlemen v. Players fixture was held.

The settings of the most prestigious clubs like Merion CC were palatial, with grand

*Lord Brackley's MCC XI which toured West Indies in 1904–05, a
predominantly amateur affair. Standing: H.V. Hesketh-Pritchard, Sir Roland
Burn, Moss (umpire), G.T. Simpson-Hayward, C.H.M. Ebden, Bellamy
(umpire), A.W.F. Somerset, Sain, G.H. Drummond; seated: G.J. Thompson,
Capt. E.G. Wynyard, Lord Brackley, C.P. Foley, E.G. Hayes.*

pavilions and space for crowds of 20,000 who appeared for matches against touring sides.
As Rowland Bowen described, mentioning the flow of sides from England:

Twelve teams from these islands made tours of North America and chiefly to
Philadelphia, and these included Kent, the first county to tour abroad, the MCC, and
many of the leading players of the time, Ranji among them. It was an extremely
pleasant ending to a cricket season to cross the Atlantic in early or mid-September and
play on till October in the marvellous surroundings to be found there. There were
three Australian tours, official in 1896 (when they managed to lose to Philadelphia in
one of their matches by an innings) and 1912, and unofficial but hardly less powerful in
1913. And Philadelphia was never found to be playing above its class.

Such was the reputation of Philadelphia cricket that when the Gentlemen of
Philadelphia first visited England in 1897 their matches were given first-class status by

Warner's XI that toured North America in 1897 played their most important games in Philadelphia, but also found time to visit Niagara Falls.

the MCC. The courteous behaviour of the visitors was exemplified at the end of the tour when, after an article had been published in a Philadelphian paper attacking the English umpiring as unfair, G.S. Patterson, the team's captain, quickly published a letter deploring the article and distancing himself and his team from such unsporting sentiments. Although the visitors enjoyed limited success, the tour revealed to English spectators the bowling of John Barton King, the outstanding player produced by Philadelphia and considered by all who saw him as one of the best bowlers of the period. *Wisden* commented somewhat dampeningly that, 'the excitement caused by accounts of King making the ball swerve in the air after the manner of the baseball pitchers soon died away', but at Hove King touched the heights. Clean bowling Ranji — at this time approaching his most brilliant form — for nought with the first delivery that he faced, King went on to take seven for 13 and Sussex were dismissed for 46. Six foot three inches

*John Barton King, Philadelphia's outstanding player and a bowler in the top
league during the Edwardian era.*

tall, King bowled medium-fast and there is no doubt that he was a pioneer of swerve
bowling.

On the two tours of 1903 and 1908 the Gentlemen of Philadelphia won seven matches
and lost six and provided good competition for the county sides. There was no doubt that
King was far and away their best player, for in addition to his bowling he was one of the

*The ground of Merion CC, Philadelphia, where cricket was played in
surroundings of splendour and affluence.*

leading batsmen, as he demonstrated most forcefully in 1903 when, against Surrey at The Oval he made 98 and 113, and at the end of the tour had amassed nearly 800 runs. It was the last tour in 1908, however, that saw King at his most successful a bowler, and at the end of the season he had taken 87 first-class wickets at an average of 11.01 which put him at the top of the English averages. It was an extraordinary feat which marked the zenith of Philadelphia's cricketing achievements. The last match of international significance to be played in Philadelphia was in 1912 when the home side defeated the Australians returning home from the Triangular Tournament in England.

Lacking the deep roots of the game in England, cricket in Philadelphia was fashionable and popular for this short period because it was ideally suited to social conditions at the time, but those conditions did not survive the war, and with the changes that came after 1918 the demise of cricket on the scale that it had been played by the Edwardians was inevitable. The teams of the 1890s and early 1900s were not replaced by new young players and the rapid spread of baseball which was easier and cheaper to establish and required less time to be played confirmed that, while this would become entrenched as a national game, cricket would be confined to being the pastime of a limited minority. The changes in fashion were clearly demonstrated by the emergence of tennis as a social game and where thousands had once watched Jessop, Ranji and many of the other leading Edwardian personalities at the Longwood and Merion clubs, by the 1920s their superbly maintained turf had been turned over to the alternative game.

9

SOME MATCHES

When the Gentlemen of Philadelphia paid their first visit to England in 1897 one of their earliest games was against Cambridge at Fenner's. Here they came up against a rather older undergraduate than usual, G.L. Jessop, who hit 140 in just over 100 minutes including some monumental blows as described by Gerald Brodribb:

> The innings lasted only 105 minutes and included two remarkable hits off H.P. Baily, the chief slow bowler. In his first over, Jessop hit him into the road by the entrance gate, an enormous hit, whereupon Baily asked to be transferred to the other end where the boundary was longer. This was done, and to the vast amusement of his fellows, Baily's first ball from that end was hit clean over the distant wall into the grounds of a girls' school.

Brodribb adds that 'any hit out of Fenner's is extremely rare'.

Jessop had finished his schooling at Cheltenham Grammar School at the early age of 15, and at that time there was no thought of him attending university. Moved to become a priest, however, he went up to Cambridge to read classics in 1896, by which time he was 22. It soon became clear that Jessop was not going to develop a sufficient grasp of the Greek language to gain his degree and his aspirations towards taking the cloth were, perforce, abandoned. But if his career as a classicist and a cleric foundered, his cricket blossomed. After his introduction to the Gloucestershire side in 1894, his years at Cambridge saw him gain a blue in four consecutive seasons and, in his last year of 1899, captain the university and make his début for England.

As Brodribb says, 1897 was the year that Jessop 'arrived'. The Philadelphians got an early taste of what had become, by the end of the season, regular fare from Jessop's bat, and a similar dose a few weeks afterwards when he scored his first hundred for Gloucestershire against them. But the highlight came at the end of July against Yorkshire on the small Harrogate ground where, on the first of many occasions, Jessop hit his way into the record books in whirlwind fashion. Although Gloucestershire were not one of Yorkshire's major opponents, the north-countrymen never took any chances and fielded a formidable bowling attack, which on the first morning had reduced the visitors to 72 for three when Jessop came in twenty minutes before lunch. At the interval he had scored 43 out of 54 runs added. Suitably revived he reappeared to add 58 out of 64 and take his

*Hastings, the scene of enjoyable festival cricket and some of Jessop's most
explosive innings.*

score to 101 when he was bowled by Stanley Jackson, one of six bowlers who had been
employed against Jessop. He had been in for 40 minutes and it was the fastest 100 ever
scored. Only Percy Fender, who scored 100 in 35 minutes for Surrey against
Northamptonshire in 1920 has bettered Jessop's rate. At one stage Jessop hit 33 runs off
eight consecutive balls, the last four bowled by George Hirst, which were dispatched for
three fours and a six.

Jessop's name dominates fast-scoring records in an astonishing manner. His 14
centuries scored in 60 minutes or less represent over 20 per cent of the total list and,
perhaps more impressive, of the five double-hundreds of his career, four are amongst the
select group of 14 to have been made in 150 minutes or less. No other batsman's name
appears more than once. Of all these scores the innings which came closest to the pace of
his Harrogate performance – and at times exceeded it – was made at Hastings in 1907 for
the Gentlemen of the South against the Players of the South, a regular fixture at the
Hastings September festival. Ironically, the change in the law which gave a six for any hit
pitching over the boundary – rather than right out of the ground – came a few years too
late for Jessop's statistical record, although it would have been of little importance to
him. By the old law he made 191 in 90 minutes, which would have been well over 200
with the new law and far and away the fastest double-hundred in history.

Jessop had made something of a name for himself at Hastings with a number of innings
before 1907. In all he hit four hundreds in under an hour on that ground. They were
mainly for representative sides during games when, with the county championship
settled and the season nearly over, if the atmosphere may have been somewhat relaxed,
the competition never lost its edge. He had already made 119 in less than an hour for

Gloucestershire against Sussex on the ground in 1907, so his appearance for the Gentlemen of the South in the festival was keenly awaited.

To groans of disappointment all round the boundary, he was bowled second ball for nought in the first innings. In the second, with his side 25 for three, he more than made up for this rare lapse. From the very first ball he attacked mercilessly and, with the crowd in virtual uproar, raced to 100 in 42 minutes and 150 in 64 minutes before being caught on the boundary for 191, made in 90 minutes. Balls were dispatched through shop windows and house windows, and thumped regularly into the walls of a neighbouring chapel. Sussex's A.E. Relf at one stage fancied his chances of getting Jessop out and asked confidently to be put on to bowl. He had one over whose six balls gave Jessop 26 runs. Most descriptions of the match were lost for superlatives, but at least the local paper kept things in proportion, concluding that, 'an otherwise insignificant match was redeemed by some bright play by Jessop'.

Among the Yorkshire players bombarded by Jessop at Harrogate in 1897 were the county's opening batsmen, J.T. Brown and J. Tunnicliffe, both John. Only Surrey, with Hayward and Abel, had an opening pair who could rival Brown and Tunnicliffe for their consistency and skill, and together they played a decisive role in Yorkshire's run of championship victories around the turn of the century. They could not have looked more different when walking out to bat: Brown was very short and stocky, built in the mould of George Hirst, while at over 6ft 2ins 'Long John', as Tunnicliffe was always known, was one of the tallest players in the game. The partnership was brought to a sadly premature end in 1904, when Brown died, aged 35, from asthma and heavy smoking.

In 1897 the two had already established a new first-wicket partnership record of 378 against Sussex in front of an approving home crowd at Sheffield, when Brown had made 311, but this was exceeded within a few weeks by Hayward and Abel who went one run

J.T. Brown (left), the only man to hit two triple-hundreds for Yorkshire, and his quite opposite partner 'Long John' Tunnicliffe, Lord Hawke's trusted senior pro of many years.

better against Hampshire at home at The Oval. In 1898 the two Yorkshiremen settled the matter once and for all, and in the process 'christened' their neighbouring county Derbyshire's new ground at Queen's Park, Chesterfield – only a few miles south of Sheffield in an area where county rivalry was keen – which had been laid out the previous season to celebrate Queen Victoria's Golden Jubilee. The home side were embarking upon a lean period in their fortunes and the relentless amassing of runs by the two Yorkshiremen did nothing for their morale. At the end of the first day they had made 503 with Brown 270 not out and Tunnicliffe 214. Shortly before lunch the next day Tunnicliffe was out on 243 when the partnership stood at 554, a total exceeded only once in England, by their fellow-Yorkshiremen Holmes and Sutcliffe, in 1932.

Brown went on to score 300 before giving away his wicket and his greater share of the runs reflected the balance of their partnership, for he was one of the greatest batsmen to have been produced by Yorkshire, and the dominant, more stylish figure. 'Long John' Tunnicliffe disciplined his naturally aggressive batting to produce a more controlled and reliable style. If Sir Home Gordon is to be believed, it is probable that Tunnicliffe spent the Sunday of the match speaking at a Baptist or Methodist chapel in Chesterfield for he was 'an earnest Nonconformist, who generally preached in some local chapel when his side were on tour'. Certainly alcohol never passed his lips, and it was as much these personal qualities as his cricketing ability which led Lord Hawke to choose him as the county's senior pro for many years.

When Brown and Tunnicliffe made their record partnership at Chesterfield, Yorkshire went on to score 662 and demolish Derbyshire by an innings and 387 runs, but a few years later, in 1904, the home side triumphed on the ground against Essex in one of the most remarkable matches in the history of the county championship. Essex batted first and by the end of the first day had amassed 597 with P.A. Perrin, who had gone in first wicket down, the not-out batsman with 343, including 68 fours, still a world record.

Given Derbyshire's reputation, an Essex victory seemed assured but, batting through the second day and into the morning of the third, Derbyshire replied with 548. Most of the side scored runs but the innings was dominated by C.A. Ollivierre (who had stayed in

QUEEN'S PARK, CHESTERFIELD.

JULY 18, 19, and 20, 1904. Stumps Drawn at 6-30.

DERBYSHIRE v. ESSEX.

ESSEX.

	First Innings		Second Innings	
1 P L Fane	lbw, b Curgenven	63	b Warren	2
2 Carpenter	b Bestwick	5	c Warren, b Bestwick	2
3 P Perrin	not out	343	c & b Warren	8
4 P McGahey	b Bestwick	32	c Cadman, b Bestwick	5
5 Rev F H Gillingham	c and b Warren	43	absent	
6 Sewell	b Warren	10	c Cadman, b Curgenven	41
7 Reeves	b Warren	0	b Bestwick	0
8 R P Keigwin	lbw, b Ashcroft	14	b Needham, b Warren	0
9 J W H T Douglas	b Ollivierre	47	not out	27
10 Russell, B	c Humphries, b Cadman	23	b Curgenven	0
11 Buckenham	lbw, b Bestwick	3	b Warren	8
	byes 2 lb 5 wds 3 nb 4	14	bys 1 lb 1 wds 2 nb 1	4
	Total	**597**	**Total**	**97**

Fall of Wickets—1st Inns.

1	2	3	4	5	6	7	8	9	10
12	132	179	300	314	314	383	534	586	597

2nd Inns.

| 4 | 4 | 17 | 21 | 21 | 26 | 83 | 83 | 97 | .. |

BOWLING ANALYSIS.

	O	M	R	W	O	M	R	W
Warren	29	3	143	3	16.1	5	42	4
Bestwick	42.1	8	160	3	16	4	34	3
Cadman	22	3	65	1	2	0	10	0
Storer	7	0	41	0	..	..	..	..
Curgenven	16	1	67	1	5	2	7	2
Ashcroft	7	1	38	1	..	..	..	0
Morton	8	1	39	0	..	..	..	0
Wright	4	0	15	0	..	..	..	0
Ollivierre	3	0	15	1	..	..	..	0

DERBYSHIRE.

	First Innings		Second Innings	
1 Mr L G Wright	c Fane, b Reeves	68	c Carpenter, b Buckenham	1
2 Mr C A Ollivierre	b Reeves	229	not out	92
3 Storer	b Buckenham	44	not out	48
4 Mr E M Ashcroft	b Sewell	34		
5 Needham	b Reeves	47		
6 Mr G Curgenven	b Buckenham	51		
7 Morton	b Reeves	16		
8 Cadman	c Douglas, b Reeves	34		
9 Warren	b Douglas	18		
10 Humphries	not out	2		
11 Bestwick	lbw, b Douglas	0		
	byes 6 lb 18 wds 1 nb	25	bys 4 lb 2 wds 1 nb 1	8
	Total	**548**	**Total**	**149**

Umpires—
W Wright & S Brown

Fall of Wickets—1st Inns.

1	2	3	4	5	6	7	8	9	10
191	319	375	410	462	478	499	530	544	548

2nd Inns.

1	2								
11	..	..	..	..	..	..	..	..	..

BOWLING ANALYSIS.

	O	M	R	W	O	M	R	W
Buckenham	43	5	176	2	13	0	78	1
Keigwin	7	1	36	0				
Reeves	51	7	192	5	13	1	43	0
Douglas	15.3	1	54	2	2	0	14	0
McGahey	11	2	34	0	2	1	6	0
Sewell	7	0	31	1	..	..	..	0

Printed on the Ground by S. B. Smith, of Back Sitwell-street, Derby

The scorecard for Derbyshire's dramatic win over Essex.

England and qualified for Derbyshire after touring with the 1900 West Indies side), who scored 229. The rest of the last day saw mounting excitement when, having dismissed Essex for 97 in their second innings, the home side were roared on towards the target of 149 with only an hour and a half to make the runs. They did so for the loss of only one wicket, Ollivierre again the hero with 92 not out.

Peter Perrin, as he was known by his friends despite his Christian names of Percival

Peter Perrin, one of many Essex characters.

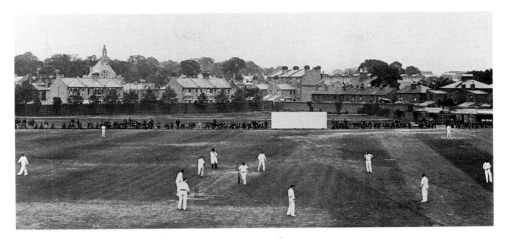

*The ground at Leyton, Essex's headquarters in east
London throughout the Edwardian era.*

Albert, was the outstanding batsman in an Essex side dominated by amateurs throughout the period, largely because, like a number of the lesser and poorer counties, they could not afford to pay a large staff of regular professionals. Of only five amateurs who appeared consistently in every season from 1895 to 1914, two of them – C.P. McGahey and F.L. Fane – played for Essex. With their headquarters at Leyton they were a distinctly east London side, quite different from the more refined and prosperous county club of today, based in Chelmsford.

Perrin, who only missed the first year of the period and played consistently from 1896, was born in Hackney, as was Charlie McGahey, who usually followed Perrin in the batting order at number four. They formed the mainstay of the county's batting and gave it a well-deserved reputation for being entertaining – at least until the appearance of Johnnie Douglas. Both Perrin and McGahey stood well over six feet and as a result were dubbed the 'Essex twins' by the scorer at Leyton because he could not tell them apart when they were at the wicket.

Perrin and 'Cheerful Charlie' McGahey were great friends and great characters, neither of them well off but both devoted to cricket. Perrin was without question the best amateur batsman never to play for England; even more surprisingly, he never played for the Gentlemen against the Players and the reason in both cases was his deplorable fielding. These gaps, and the fact that his 343 was the highest score ever made by a batsman on a losing side, add a somewhat melancholy note to assessments of his career, but when he was batting the situation was very different. Both he and McGahey were terrific hitters, especially driving off the front foot. Perrin's forte was defying fast bowling, as he demonstrated in his first match for Essex in 1896 when, aged 19, he scored 50 at The Oval against Richardson in his prime. McGahey's best-known strength was the power of his straight driving and on one occasion he broke the arm of his unfortunate non-striking partner at the bowler's end.

Between the wars Perrin became one of the shrewdest and most conscientious of Test selectors, while McGahey, who was at different times during his playing career both captain and assistant secretary, the latter position to provide him with a much-needed salary, retained strong links with Essex as the county's scorer from 1930. The most obvious difference between the two was that, while Perrin was a strict teetotaller, McGahey would never refuse a drink and for a time lived at a pub in Leyton. Perrin himself once recalled a match when they were batting together and McGahey, on 99, called for a quick single but was bowled. As he passed the bowler on his way back to the pavilion he grinned and told him, 'Luckily for you I wanted a drink'. In *Background of Cricket*, Sir Home Gordon recounted a story of McGahey returning home from a match by train and sharing his compartment with an elderly Essex supporter who remarked,

> 'Sorry to see young Perrin get out: pity he lifts his elbow. I always know whether he is fit or not.'
> McGahey retorted, 'You don't mean Perrin, you mean McGahey.'
> 'I don't, for I know Perrin quite well,' rather crossly.
> 'Well, McGahey says you don't mean Perrin, you mean me, I am McGahey. Perrin is a teetotaller and all the drink he refuses, I take.'

It was Charlie McGahey who was responsible for R.C. Robertson-Glasgow's nickname of 'Crusoe'. Playing in one of his last matches for Essex after the war, against Oxford in the Parks, he was bowled by Robertson-Glasgow and returned to the pavilion to be asked by Johnny Douglas how he had been out. 'I was bowled by an old bugger I thought had been dead for two thousand years called Robinson Crusoe.'

As well as these two, the Essex amateurs included some of the richest personalities of the period, although their efforts rarely brought them anywhere near contention for honours in the county championship. Most endearing was Canon F.H. Gillingham, a tall elegant batsman who was, for much of the period, a curate in the largely impoverished Leyton parish where he joined in games of street cricket with the local urchins, and later became chaplain to King George VI. Most widely known – and feared – was C.J. Kortright, acknowledged to be the fastest bowler of the Edwardian era. He was also one of the most combative and had no qualms about attacking batsmen mercilessly, especially if he had some sort of grievance against them. Around the turn of the century many people limped off at Leyton bruised and shaken by an assault from 'Korty'. Not least because of his fearsome attacks in many Gentlemen v. Players matches the professional batsmen were unanimous in their respect for Kortright, which was perfectly expressed by Johnny Tyldesley when he was once asked whether Kortright 'did anything with the ball'. 'No, he just bowled fast – there wasn't time for anything else.'

Kortright was no longer bombarding the Players in 1906 when the centenary of Gentlemen v. Players matches at Lord's was marked by devastating fast bowling on both sides. As H.S. Altham wrote, 'With the exception of one wicket that fell to J.N. Crawford and one run out the whole forty wickets were accounted for by three genuine fast bowlers, Knox, Brearley and Fielder and by Walter Lees, who was distinctly quicker than medium.' In the first innings of the game Kent's Arthur Fielder made

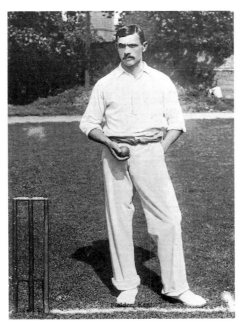

*Arthur Fielder of Kent, who took all ten Gentlemen's
wickets in 1906.*

history when he took all ten of the Gentlemen's wickets – the only time it was ever done
in all Gentlemen v. Players matches – to skittle them out for 167. In reply for the
Gentlemen, Surrey's N.A. Knox and Lancashire's Walter Brearley were if anything more
ferocious, and between them dismissed the Players for 199. The batting highlight of the
match came in the Gentlemen's second innings when Reggie Spooner, going in first,
scored 114 with an easy elegance that only he could command, while the innings was
closed by Jessop in equally characteristic style, racing to 73 not out with the total at 321.
Needing 290 to win, the Players were soon in trouble against the pace of Knox who took
seven for 110 to give his side victory by 45 runs. In his meteoric career of seven seasons
Knox was second only to Kortright as the fastest amateur bowler of the period, and his
fellow Surrey player Jack Hobbs concluded that he was, 'I think, the best fast bowler I
ever saw'.

Because of the wealth of talent available to both sides, the quality of play in Gentlemen
v. Players matches throughout the Edwardian era touched heights never attained either
before or since, and while the Players easily dominated the results taken as a whole, this
was the only period when the Gentlemen regularly held their own. Three years before
the bowlers' match of 1906 amateur batting enjoyed one of its most majestic exhibitions
when, on the last day of the 1903 game, the Gentlemen turned round a seemingly
hopeless situation. In reply to the Players' first innings of 478 they were bowled out for
185 and followed on 293 runs behind. After Warner was out, shortly after the start of

play on the third morning, Ranji joined Fry and the Sussex pair embarked upon a miraculous revival of the Gentlemen's fortunes by adding 142 in an hour and a half until Ranji was out for 60. Fry was then joined by Archie MacLaren and in something less than three hours the two simply brushed aside the Players' bowling to add 309 runs before MacLaren declared at 500, when they were both still in. He had made 168 and Fry 232, the highest score ever in these games at Lord's. Given the display they had put on, most of the spectators forgot that they had originally been saving a doomed match and the outcome of a draw was irrelevant. Many years afterwards Cardus wrote that, 'never has such batsmanship been seen as this for opulence and prerogative'.

The years around the turn of the century were, in terms of English cricket, dominated by two features, the batting of Ranji and Fry for Sussex and the supremacy of Yorkshire in the county championship. So huge were the aggregate of runs amassed by the two batsmen and the accompanying averages that the figures on their own almost fail to convey the inevitability of their scoring. Certainly the occasions on which they both made large scores – and if one failed the other almost inevitably succeeded – were so numerous that to single out specific matches is invidious. But as good an example as any came after their three most prolific years, 1899–1901, late in the 1902 season when after weeks of wet weather the sun finally came out and allowed batsmen to perform on good wickets. The game against Surrey at Hastings also illustrates the huge scores that were so often amassed on good wickets, because sides were compelled by the declaration law to bat on well into the second day. In Sussex's first innings they scored 419 runs on the first day, Fry making 159 and sharing in a first-wicket partnership with Joe Vine who was first out for 92. In came Ranji who had made 54 by the close of play. The next day he went to 234 and was still in when he declared at 705 for eight. Surrey responded in a similar manner, so that nearly a thousand runs were scored on the first two days, and when the match ended in a draw they had made 552 with their first three batsmen all making hundreds.

Yorkshire's inexorable progress during these years had one totally unexpected setback which came in July 1901. The county had been champions in 1898, slipped to third in 1899, and then regained their rightful place for the next three successive seasons. Having gone unbeaten throughout 1900, they retained the record through 1901 until they had played 43 consecutive games without loss – and won 13 by an innings and 4 by ten wickets. Then they met Somerset at Leeds and the great run was ended. Many observers could not contain their astonishment but Somerset, despite never having sufficient depth to their teams to enjoy consistent success, had shown themselves to be specialist giant-killers ever since their first season as a first-class county when they routed the champions, Surrey. The best account of the game was written by Sammy Woods, who had declined as a bowler but was the county's captain, which, as well as describing the action, gives a delightful flavour of this revered Somerset figure.

We had our historic game at Leeds in the middle of July. I must say at once that the two great Yorkshire bowlers, Hirst and Rhodes, had been very hard worked, as, if I remember rightly, Haigh who had been so deadly the year before, was not of much use on the hard wickets that we had this year. However, for many years afterwards he was

SAMMY :—" Better be drowned in Somerset cider than Lancashire beer. It is more soothing."

Somerset's extraordinary win over Yorkshire was celebrated by 'Rip' of the
Evening News, the best newspaper cartoonist of the period.

as good as ever, and, of course, Wainwright, their other bowler, was best on bad
wickets. So Hirst and Rhodes had a bellyful of bowling. Yorkshire had gone unbeaten
until we met them, and I expect they were quite pleased to be beaten at last and the
tension taken off their nerves.

It was a curious match in many ways. To start with it was a fiery wicket from start
to finish. I won the toss and went in. We were all out for 87; a godchild of mine whom
I had sent for as we were one short (not an unusual thing for us) got 11 and I got 46.
Yorkshire then went in and got 325; Hirst 61, Haigh 96, Rhodes 44, all their bowlers
getting runs. They played very well, as we had a fine fast bowler, Gill, who ought to
have bowled them out for 150. Still he did not, and so the first day ended with
Yorkshire leading by 238 runs on the first innings.

Four of us, Palairet, Hill, Phillips and myself, had dinner with Mr Hepworth, Mayor
or ex-Mayor of Leeds, and a very good dinner, too. When it came to the liqueur stakes

he informed us the brandy was the best in the land. I said 'Right oh! The best is good enough for us.' I remember it was produced in half-bottles. Only one came at first, and tiny liqueur glasses. When I said it tasted better out of claret glasses some more quickly arrived. Presently he said that if Somerset won he would give £100 to the county funds. I never got it. Still I won £10 over the game as I took 10 to 1 Palairet got a hundred, which, of course, he did.

Next morning Palairet and Braund started scoring at once and soon got the upper hand of the bowling. There was an appeal against Braund for a catch at slip by Tunnicliffe. Neither umpire could see it. I did, and could not tell if it hit the ground or not. Still, John Tunnicliffe always maintains it was a catch. These two put on well over 200 for the first wicket. The bowlers got tired, especially George Hirst. Phillips strained his leg and I ran for him for about 80 runs (he got 120). I said to Hirst 'Are you tired?' He said, 'Yes, my feet are so sore I can hardly run up to the wicket.' Hill 53, Robson 40 and myself 66, went on with the good work. Of course I was sorry for the bowlers, still it would be a change for the whole team to have a good day's scouting and they did stick to it. As I said before, we were generally the side to show the public how to field, or rather how not to do so.

Next day we got them out for 118, and so won by 279 runs. Braund and Cranfield bowled very well, and our catching was quite good for a change. We had a great reception after the game. The vast crowd cheered themselves hoarse, and, as I always have maintained, there are no better sportsmen in the world than the Yorkshire crowd.

Woods's reference to the reaction of the Yorkshire crowd confirms his boundless generosity and good nature which combined with his gargantuan appetite for life. Certainly a few glasses of brandy would have had no adverse effect: towards the end of his life he said, 'There is one thing I have steadily tried to do; to drink more beer for the years I have lived than any other man who has ever come down from Cambridge.' Freshly arrived from his native Australia, it was as an undergraduate at Cambridge that he first displayed his cricketing ability, especially his fast bowling which was at its best during these years, and his appetite. During a match against C.I. Thornton's XI he and his close friend the university wicket-keeper, Gregor MacGregor, invited some of the opposition to breakfast in their rooms at Jesus College on the second morning of the match. The scene is described by Sir Home Gordon who wrote of Woods, 'grey matter not being predominant in his powerful physique'.

They [the visitors] clamoured for bacon and eggs with tea, instead of the hot lobster and tankard of beer put before each of them. So Sammy ate all the lobsters, drank all the beer and then proceeded to take all ten wickets: 'Just to show that a little nourishment is not harmful' as he explained to P.J. de Paravicini.

Woods was usually unstinting in his praise of other cricketers but two members of his Somerset side were always singled out. Lionel Palairet he regarded with the kind of profound respect and admiration usually reserved for deities, while Len Braund was 'the

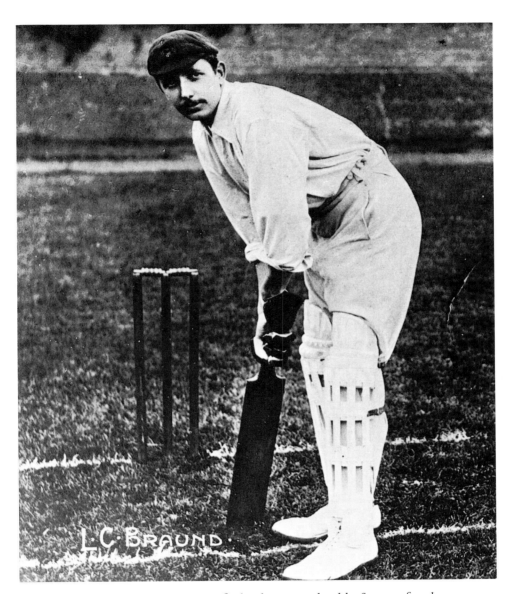

*Len Braund, reviled by Surrey for his desertion, adored by Somerset for whom
his all-round skill proved invaluable.*

best all-round cricketer who ever played for Somerset'. The summer of 1901 was
Braund's first full season for Somerset and from then until 1914 they would have often
been lost without him. As much as anything his arrival delighted Woods because he
deserted the latter's arch-enemies, Surrey, for whom he never showed the form he was

to do – as opening bat, bowler and fielder – for Somerset. Surrey soon realized what they had lost and were so piqued that when another player, Montgomery, not half as good as Braund and who only played ten games for Somerset, followed the same path in 1904 they cancelled their fixtures with Somerset and refused to reinstate them until 1907.

The summer of 1907 was a miserable one, dominated by rain, and as a result bowlers took advantage of the conditions to, for once, assert superiority over the batsmen. Up and down the country they amassed impressive hauls of wickets while batsmen struggled to make runs. Charlie Blythe took 17 wickets in one day against Northamptonshire and 15 in the Second Test against the South Africans. Gloucestershire's E.G. Dennett took 15 wickets in both his county's matches against the luckless Northamptonshire, and George Hirst took 15 Leicestershire wickets for Yorkshire at Hull.

The county championship was won by a pair of bowlers, Wass and Hallam of Nottinghamshire, and decided at Lord's against Middlesex in the match immediately after the sensation of the season, caused by Lancashire's captain Archie MacLaren. MacLaren had brought the Lancashire side down to Lord's for their game against Middlesex which, although only just over two hours of play took place during the entire three days, was discussed in furious terms for months afterwards. Rain on the first day delayed the start until mid-afternoon, and Lancashire only had time to make 57 runs before they were again driven off by the weather. The next morning more rain had submerged the pitch and the umpires announced that no play would be possible that day. A number of the spectators were none too happy with the decision and, on their way to object in front of the pavilion, many of them passed close to or over the wicket. They were placated by an assurance that they would be allowed in on the last day without further charge, but the damage had been done. MacLaren issued a terse statement which read, 'Owing to the pitch having been deliberately torn up by the public, I, as captain of the Lancashire eleven, cannot see my way to continue the game, the groundsman bearing me out that the wicket could not be again put right.'

Even by the standards of MacLaren's well-known high-handedness, it was an extraordinary course of action and universally condemned. W.G. Grace and Warner were just two of the cricket heavyweights who subsequently condemned his action in letters to the press. Most people considered that he had coerced the groundsman and forced his will upon the umpires. His stance was further objected to the next day when, while the Lancashire side did not even turn up at the ground, the pitch was rolled into a state which was reckoned to be easily playable. It was a reflection of MacLaren's reputation that, despite never being on the best of terms with the MCC authorities at Lord's, they did not take the opportunity to reprimand him and the match was just abandoned as a draw.

About the only national publication to come out in support of MacLaren was his home county's *Manchester Guardian* which gave a spirited account of the second day's events and reserved their criticism for the MCC authorities and the club's secretary, F.E. Lacey.

It was a most irritating day for all concerned. The sky was overcast but no rain fell, while the outfield, which is less heavily and much less frequently rolled than the 'pitch', was quite firm. In the absence of sun and wind, however, the pitch hardly dried at all, and presented all day a glutinous look peculiar to the ground. Under the circumstances play was out of the question, for neither the batsmen nor the bowlers could have secured a proper footing. Why people should have been admitted with the ground unfit for play and with but little prospect of play is best known to the Lord's authorities. In any case upwards of a thousand persons paid for admission. These endured with commendable patience the weary wait before lunch in the hope that play would begin after the midday meal. When it became obvious that there was no intention of making a start the spectators became indignant, and for the rest of the afternoon made a series of angry demonstrations in front of the pavilion.

At first the spectators were content to gather in groups and discuss their wrongs. But a leader is usually forthcoming under such circumstances. In the present instance he appeared in the person of a rather excited gentleman, who, after addressing the crowd, led them in a loud-voiced chorus of 'We want play', which was repeated at intervals. He also delivered several speeches in front of the pavilion and seemed to have the crowd under his control.

Mr Lacey, the MCC secretary, appeared to be in doubt as to what course to take, but eventually he went out amongst the crowd and informed them that they would receive checks admitting to the ground to-day in the event of no play taking place. This pacified the crowd for a time. When, however, the umpires went out for a final inspection and drew the stumps, this tacit intimation that play had been abandoned for the day led to a demonstration without parallel at Lord's. The umpires, on their way back to the pavilion with the stumps, were followed by a hooting and yelling mob. The umpires were escorted only by two policemen. No violence was offered to them, but they were hooted and abused as the arbiters who had decided against play. Once the umpires had reached the pavilion the crowd turned and stampeded over the pitch, the protecting ropes being ignored, while the groundsmen, in the absence of police, were unable to prevent the more unconscionable section of the crowd from venting their wrath on the offending wicket.

The paper concluded:

Whether MacLaren took the right or wrong course must remain a matter of opinion, but it is beyond dispute that the authorities at headquarters contributed to this most unhappy 'sensation' by taking money at the gates when well aware that play was very improbable. At The Oval money is not taken and the gates are not opened unless there is some prospect of play being clearly practicable.

Possibly the upheavals of the first three days of the week played their part in Middlesex's failure in the subsequent three when they played Nottinghamshire. Until the match, both sides were unbeaten and vying for supremacy in the first two places of the county championship. As was the pattern throughout the season Nottinghamshire's bowling partnership of Wass and Hallam proved decisive and in a desperate finish the visitors succeeded by 13 runs. Thereafter Middlesex declined and lost three more matches while Nottinghamshire remained unbeaten. The sustained effort of the two

*'Ted' Alletson, whose one blazing moment of glory in
1911 assured him a place in cricket legend.*

bowlers was heroic by any standards: they accounted for 298 out of the total of 340
wickets taken by Nottinghamshire during the summer, they bowled out county sides for
under 100 on 13 occasions, and by the end of the season they had bowled unchanged
during 11 innings.

It was another Nottinghamshire player, Edwin Boaler Alletson, who stepped briefly
into the Edwardian limelight in 1911 to secure for himself a place in cricket legend.
'Ted' Alletson was born and lived on the Duke of Portland's huge estate outside Worksop
in the north of the county and, like his father, worked down one of his Grace's many
coal-mines. He first played for Nottinghamshire in 1906 and, although he stood well over
six foot, weighed $15\frac{1}{2}$ stone and was enormously strong, never did anything out of the
ordinary as a batsman or bowler. That was until he travelled to Brighton in May 1911, to
play Sussex at Hove, traditionally a favourite excursion for the Nottinghamshire men
and, for some of them, the only time they ever saw the seaside.

By the last morning of the match the visitors might have enjoyed their stay at the
Regency resort, but their chances of avoiding defeat in the match seemed hopeless.
When Alletson went in at number nine their lead was nine runs and if, as was widely
expected, Sussex took the remaining wickets cheaply before lunch they would have the
rest of the day to knock off the modest number of runs required. For some reason the
spirit moved Alletson, otherwise it is difficult to account for his behaviour. Not only did

he ask his captain Jones whether he could 'have a go', but when Jones concurred, feeling that there was no harm as their cause was as good as lost anyway, Alletson apparently muttered as he left the pavilion, 'Then I'm not half going to give Tom Killick some stick.'

His progress before lunch was modest compared to what was to come, but rather than the fact that he scored 47 in 50 minutes, most onlookers were surprised that he was still in. One cannot help speculating as to what Alletson consumed at lunchtime because immediately afterwards his onslaught began. In 40 minutes he scored 142 runs off 51 balls and if he was undiscriminating in his attack, Killick certainly bore the brunt of it: 22 off one over and 34 off another, the poor bowler being in such a state by this time that he sent down two no-balls and Alletson gratefully scored boundaries (4664446) off seven of the eight balls offered. He was attended by the last man Bill Riley who contributed ten runs to Alletson's 142, although his chances were few and far between. Of Alletson's 189, 140 came in boundaries, 8 sixes and 23 fours, so he kept tight control of the strike.

What players and spectators alike most remembered about the innings was how hard Alletson hit the ball and, towards the end when his scoring seemed to build up into a crescendo, the Sussex fielders were more concerned with getting out of the ball's way rather than trying to stop it. Cyril Foley, who was among the spectators, described the innings in his memoirs, and although some of his descriptions are, as could be expected, somewhat fanciful, he did paint a vivid picture when speculating how many more runs Alletson would have scored had not so much time been lost finding replacements for the balls which he dispatched irretrievably out of the ground. 'Also time was wasted in trying to prise one ball out of the new stand into whose soft wood Alletson had driven it, no chisel being available.'

And so what had begun as a peaceful day at Hove with little promise of excitement and a generally predictable outcome produced one of the sensations of the period. News of Alletson's innings spread fast, and his appearance was subsequently anticipated with huge excitement at county grounds.

But that was it; as Cyril Foley went on to describe:

After these fireworks, his appearance at Lord's against Middlesex was keenly anticipated. An enormous crowd assembled to see him. He certainly made a fair score, including a gigantic on-drive over the clock, but was otherwise disappointing. From then onwards he retired into his shell and absolutely refused to hit.

Later in the season I went to see him at The Oval, and happened to sit in the Nottinghamshire dressing-room next to A.O. Jones, the Notts skipper. 'Jonah' was in despair. He said to me: 'The man can't be normal. I've told him that I will play him in every match all through the season even if he makes recurrent cyphers, *as long as he'll hit*, but he just won't do it. You'll see for yourself presently.' And I did. In came Alletson with a huge crowd on tiptoe with excitement and made the most scratchy 11 runs possible. Never once did he attempt to hit the ball.

Disappointment thereafter or not, nothing would detract from Ted Alletson's one blaze of glory, for which the Duke of Portland gave him a gold watch and his father gave him a ham from a home-raised pig.

10

SOCIAL CRICKET

The sixth Duke of Portland who rewarded Ted Alletson so generously for his exploits at Hove was more enthusiastic about racing than cricket – in fact he was one of the most successful owners of the Edwardian period. But one of his noble cousins, the fifteenth Duke of Norfolk, made his own lavish contribution to the momentous cricket events of 1895 when he decided that he would like his own private ground at Arundel Castle, his ancestral seat in Sussex. Only the best would do for his Grace. Having enquired what was the largest ground in the country and been told that it was The Oval he determined that his would be the same size. Before the end of the year, 200 men had cut out an amphitheatre of three and a half acres from a hillside in the park surrounding his castle, a site which remains today one of the most picturesque grounds in England.

Not everyone could afford to do things on such a ducal scale, but many others took the creation of a cricket ground equally seriously. When Henry Hawkins, who played for Northamptonshire, decided to make a ground at his home Everdon Hall in 1899, he used his influence to persuade the groundsman at Lord's to travel to Northamptonshire to give

A far, but picturesque, outpost of country-house cricket: Ventnor on the Isle of Wight.

AUSTRALIANS *v* EARL DE LA WARR'S XI.

THE MANOR HOUSE CRICKET GROUND,
BEXHILL-ON-SEA.

Earl & Countess De La Warr
request the honor of
The Earl of Sheffield & Miss Attenborough's Company,
at Luncheon on 30 *or* 31 *July or* Aug 1 *1896,*
at 1.30 p.m.
Herr Warm's Viennese White Band will perform during the day.
Please bring this Card with you. R.S.V.P. *Entrance from Sea Road.*
For special trains &c please see railway bills

The highest echelons of cricket and society: an invitation to luncheon during the
game between the 1896 Australians and Earl de la Warr's XI.

his advice upon the details of site and the establishment of a good batting wicket. Such country-house grounds became important status symbols for Edwardian landowners who could still afford to regard their estates as places to provide social entertainment – which normally meant shooting in the winter and cricket in the summer. At a time when the upper classes had plenty of time for their leisure, when weekend parties were not interfered with by the modern phenomenon of the working week and were often more like week parties, lasting three or four days, cricket enjoyed its hey-day of social popularity.

George Cornwallis-West, a debonair member of the highest echelons of Edwardian society, whose two sisters married the Duke of Westminster and the German Prince Hans of Pless, remembered that, 'many large country houses in Edwardian days had private cricket-grounds in the park and cricket weeks in August after the London Season were most amusing. Invitations to them were eagerly accepted by those with any pretensions to playing the game.' At best the standard of play was comparable to first-class, especially at places belonging to grandees involved with county cricket, such as the Earl of Coventry's Worcestershire home Croome Court, or at Belmont Park, Lord Harris's home in Kent. Elsewhere the standard was more modest and the atmosphere less competitive, keen sons and their friends being joined by gardeners, chauffeurs and other retainers to take on their county neighbours.

Cornwallis-West played regular country-house cricket as a young man and his memoirs *Edwardian Hey-Days* contain a description which characterizes social cricket as it was played in the shires up and down the country. It also illustrates the author's eye for social detail, as well as the often unexpected characters who were attracted to the game.

> I spent many a happy cricket week at Frampton Court in Dorsetshire, the beautiful place belonging to Squire Sheridan, the direct descendant of Richard Brinsley Sheridan. I and the sons of the house – there being four in those days – started in the morning by marking and rolling the pitch, the old squire superintending. At eleven o'clock the game began. One of the two daughters of the house, who are now Lady Wavertree and Lady Stracey, usually scored. Open house was kept, and every afternoon there was a sort of informal garden-party, many neighbours turning up. It was there that I made the acquaintance of Thomas Hardy, a man who knew more about his own county and English folklore generally than anyone I have ever met.

When stumps were drawn there was usually time for Cornwallis-West and his friends to spend an hour or so fishing for trout on the River Frome before dinner, followed by dancing, every evening.

If aspiring sons were keen enough, indulgent parents would often take on a professional to coach the young hopefuls and help organize matches. It was in such circumstances that Fred Root was engaged at an impressionable age by the Countess of Warwick at Easton Lodge, her country house in Essex. Root, who was to become outspoken in his criticism of the social divides in English cricket and the lot of professional players, was still young enough to be greatly impressed by his new surroundings which, as he describes in increasingly grandiloquent terms, were a world apart from what he was accustomed to.

> Here country-house cricket was played under ideal conditions. The game was the thing the whole of the time. At any rate that seemed to be the slogan of the people invited by Lady Warwick to play in the matches. Although young in years and experience, I realized the vast difference between cricket as a game and cricket as a means to an end – that end being one's daily bread. I must admit that my healthy, youthful appetite, running in harmony with a sensible appreciation of good things, was responsible occasionally for my being very busy during the luncheon interval, and the brilliant house-parties which were from time to time arranged provided a delightful alternative to cricket matches. In those good old days Lady Warwick was one of society's greatest figures. All the noted persons of the age forgathered at her invitation, and world celebrities passed along the horizon of my admiring vision with that semi-personal contact which cricket provides. The game is a great bridge over the gulf of class distinction. Royal personages of our own court, and the courts of foreign countries, now laid in the dusty ruins of the Great War, came to Easton Lodge, and many of them crossed the Park to the cricket ground, to play or to look on.

Root recalled that he was taken on to coach Lady Warwick's younger son, The Honourable Maynard Greville, but, as the formidable hostess herself described, her eldest son Guy was equally enthusiastic about the game, and the original reason for her

*W.G. and J.R. Mason cause amusement to Lord Hawke (standing, far left) at
Hastings during the match between Yorkshire and All England in 1901.*

matches at Easton which, entertaining in the style to which she was accustomed, were
certainly social cricket on the grand scale.

> As a young man my son Guy was very keen on cricket, and in order to please him we
> used to have cricket weeks at Easton, during which we entertained large numbers of
> visitors. We used to put up at least two teams in the house, spread a big luncheon tent
> and invite the county to see the play. Various teams of the Guards, I Zingari and other
> well-known elevens would play on the ground. One summer, to the great delight and
> excitement of my son, W.G. Grace accepted an invitation to come to Easton.

Lady Warwick's meeting with W.G. prompted her to give a revealing portrait of the
great man. 'William Gilbert Grace gave me the impression of being surprised at his own
popularity. He knew, of course, that he played a good game of cricket but I do not think
he ever quite understood why he should be a national hero on that account.'

In some places cricket – like many other forms of entertainment enjoyed by the
Edwardian upper classes – was used as an excuse for a house-party and was of secondary
importance itself. For most people a balance could normally be struck quite easily and it
was rarely necessary for those who took their cricket with the utmost seriousness to go
to the precautionary lengths of the McGaw family, at their ground at St Leonard's Forest
in Sussex, which R.L. Arrowsmith once described in an essay on country-house cricket
which appeared in *Barclays World of Cricket*:

> There, there was a strictly male pavilion for the players and a comfortable stand for
> the ladies on the other side of the ground, to which those whose inclinations went that
> way or who felt a strong sense of duty to their hospitable hostess could repair; but if

*Plum Warner playing croquet under the beady eye of his wife, whose knowledge
of cricket was famous.*

you happened to be feeling somnolent after a good lunch, or to have made a duck or
even perhaps to agree with Lord Chesterfield in preferring to study men by day and
women by night, then you were welcome to stay on the less social side of the ground.

All the same, even in the most cricket-minded of households, social niceties were rarely
forgotten. One young cricketer of not inconsiderable talent was never asked to play again
by Lord Hawke after his first visit to Wighill Park when he lit a cigar while his lordship's
port was circulating the table after dinner.

Lord Hawke, not a socialite anyway, was usually too preoccupied with the affairs of
either Yorkshire or the MCC to give much attention to country-house cricket, but at
Hovingham Hall, the home of the Worsley family on the other side of York from Wighill,
the game was played to the highest standard and a number of the most illustrious names
of the period appeared. In a busy season the highlight was the August cricket week of
three two-day matches when the Hall and other houses in the vicinity were filled with
guests. Cricket was already well-established at Hovingham, but now it took on a new
lease of life, largely thanks to the enthusiasm of Sir William Worsley, third Baronet, and
his brother Arthington, and the former's son — also William — who was later to play for
and captain Yorkshire. In 1902 R.E. Foster, probably taking advantage of an invitation to
play for the Gentlemen against the Players at Scarborough a few days later, appeared at
Hovingham for a visiting local side, Whitwell Hall, and saved the match for them when
they were forced to follow on, by going in first and scoring 93. Many years later the
'young' William Worsley of those days, by now Sir William, fourth Baronet, recorded
that it was the most memorable performance in all the years' cricket at Hovingham that
he could recall. Foster had already established himself as one of the most brilliant young

amateurs, and the appearance of players with his kind of reputation hugely elevated the kudos of the country-house game.

At Hovingham there was no question that the most keenly enjoyed matches between 1902 and 1908 were the four occasions when Ranjitsinhji played on the ground. The connection arose when Ranji visited the Reverend Louis Borrisow, who as chaplain of Trinity College Cambridge had looked after and tutored Ranji, and had now retired to be Rector of East Gilling, one of the college's livings and a neighbouring parish to Hovingham. Here Ranji came to stay in successive late summers, to shoot, fish, and play cricket. In two of the matches Ranji played for Hovingham but in the other two he brought his own teams to play the home side and there was no doubting the quality of the cricket, as is shown by Ranji's XI for the first game in 1902. With characteristic generosity he had brought three of his senior Sussex professionals on the jaunt to Yorkshire: Robert Relf, Tom Killick and Fred Tate. In addition his side included the Yorkshire professional batsman David Hunter and the slow left-arm bowler Bobby Peel, V.F.S. Crawford — almost as good a hitter as his brother J.N. — and the Reverend E.B. Firth who had played as an amateur for Yorkshire.

Ranji's stays at East Gilling and his visits to Hovingham were fondly remembered for many years afterwards. As the 'Black Prince' he was regarded with considerable fascination and entered into the local folklore. On one occasion, after he had played in a match to raise money for the church clock at East Gilling and had returned to inaugurate

Top class country-house cricket: W.G. Grace's XI v. Ranji's XI at Shillinglee
Park in Sussex, 1908. Grace has Archie MacLaren on his other side, while
Ranji has one of the period's cricketing grandees — Charles de Trafford — on his.

the new clock, one lady parishioner remarked, 'Very appropriate, they've both got gold hands and a black face.' Between the wars, when Queen Mary was visiting Hovingham, one local remembered with excitement that they 'hadn't seen royalty at Hovingham since the days of the Black Prince'.

As Lady Warwick demonstrated in her description of cricket at Easton, as well as purely social sides consisting of family and friends, and the appearances of 'stars' such as Tip Foster and Ranji, the strength of country-house cricket during the period was greatly boosted by the quantity of club sides keen to arrange fixtures in suitably attractive and convivial surroundings, and the calibre of many of the players they were able to attract. One of the most prestigious, I Zingari, which had been going since 1845, played nearly half their games on country-house grounds during the Edwardian period. In some counties, in particular Kent, the connection between the country-house game, which was played on numerous grounds, and the county's first-class game was especially strong – largely thanks to the thriving club, the Band of Brothers, whose membership was limited to the county. The quality of play by BB sides ensured that there were always good amateur players available to qualify for the county and, during the years of success from 1906–14, their leading amateurs mixed county appearances with games for BB.

Like so much of the Edwardian period, however, it was the flavour of country-house cricket at the time which was its most memorable characteristic, recorded by numerous elegant pens: E.V. Lucas, Siegfried Sassoon, P.G. Wodehouse and L.P. Hartley. Of all descriptions, the most evocative is to be found in a curious work of fiction entitled *A Fish Dinner in Memison*, by a retired civil servant called E.R. Eddison.

'Time, you know, is a curious business,' said Lord Anmering, tilting his head forward a little to let the brim of his panama hat shade his eyes; for it was teatime, and the afternoon sun, from beyond the cricket field below, blazed out of cloudless blue full in their faces. 'Love of money we're told – root of all evil. Gad! I think otherwise. I think Time strikes deeper.'

Lady Southmere replenished the vacuum with one of the more long-drawn contemplative, and non-committal varieties of the inimitable transatlantic 'Aha'.

'Look at Mary,' he said. 'Look at me. If I wasn't her father: wasn't thirty-two years her senior. Wouldn't know what to do with her.'

'Well I dare say you would.'

'Easy enough when they're not your own,' he said, as they walked on slowly, coming to a halt at the top of two flights of shallow steps that led down to the field from the gardens. 'But when they are – by Jove that's the style!' The ball, from a magnificent forward drive, sailed clean over the far fence, amid shouts of applause, for six. 'If you let your boy go and smash my melon-houses, knocking about the bowling like that, I'll tell you, I'll have no more to do with him. We mustn't forget,' he said, lower again: 'she's very young. Never force the pace.'

'O but don't I just agree? And the very dearest, sweetest – '

'You know her, well as I do. No you don't though. Look there,' putting up his eye-glass to examine the telegraph board: 'eighty. Eighty: a hundred and sixty three: that's eighty-four to win. Not so bad, with only three wickets down. It's that boy of yours is

An I Zingari side of the early 1900s (above) and their attending ladies (below).

I Zingari were the oldest and most prestigious amateur club.

doing it: wonderful steady play: nice style too: like to see him make his century. . . . Would you like to come down over there: get a bit of shade?'

'I would like to do anything anybody tells me to. This is just too perfect.' She turned, before coming down the steps, to look back for a minute to the great west front of Anmering Blunds, where it ranged beyond green lawns and flower-beds and trim deep-hued hedges of clipped box and barberry and yew: long rows of mullioned windows taking the sun, whose beams seemed to have fired the very essence of the ancient brickwork to some cool-burning airy essence of gold. This wing, by Inigo Jones, was the newest part, masking from this side the original flint-built house that had been old Sir Robert Scarnside's whom Henry VIII had made first Earl of Anmering . . .

Fifty or sixty people, may be, watched the game from this western side where the tents were and garden chairs and benches, all in a cool shade of beech and chestnut and lime and sycamore that began to throw shadows far out upon the cricket field: a pleasant summer scene as any could wish, of mingled sound and silence, stir and repose: white hats and white flannels and coloured caps and blazers contrasting here and there with more formal or darker clothes: a gaiety of muslin frocks, coloured silks, gauzes and ribbons, silken parasols and picture hats: the young, the old, the middle-aged: girls, boys, men, women: some being of the house-party, some, the belongings of the eleven that had driven over with Colonel Player from Hyrnbastwick; some neighbours and acquaintances from the countryside: wives, friends, parents, sisters, cousins, aunts. Among these their host, with Lady Southmere, now threaded his way, having for each, as he passed, the just greeting, were it a word, smile, formal salutation or private joke.

'Sorry, uncle,' said Jim Scarnside, as their paths met: he on his way to the pavilion. 'Ingloriously out for three.'

'I was always told,' Lady Southmere said, 'you ought to block a yorker.'

Popular and well-attended though they usually were, country-house cricket matches

A page from the visitors' book of a cricketing country house.

were essentially private affairs. During the day – or two days – any number of people might drift in and out of the scene, coming for lunch or tea, to watch the cricket for a couple of hours in the late afternoon before staying for dinner; but, albeit often in an informal manner, they had all been invited. But the Edwardians were certainly not ones for hiding their sartorial lights under bushels, and any opportunity for display was seized upon with alacrity. In the cricket world these occasions were some of the festival matches, in particular at Scarborough in late August or early September, the week at Canterbury in August and the traditional July fixtures at Lord's: Gentlemen v. Players, Oxford v. Cambridge and, most social of all, Eton v. Harrow.

The Scarborough Festival had been founded during the 1880s by the first Earl of Londesborough, but it was from the late 1890s until 1914, with Yorkshire cricket in the ascendant, that it enjoyed its greatest years – both socially and in terms of the cricket. The essence of the play was top-class teams playing competitive but always entertaining cricket. When the Australians visited they – and other tourists – played an invitation XI selected by C.I. 'Buns' Thornton, the major figure in the festival since its initiation, who once hit A.G. Steel out of the ground over the tall Victorian houses into Trafalgar Square beyond. Other major fixtures included Lord Londesborough's (the President's) XI v. the Champion County, Gentlemen v. Players and Yorkshire v. MCC. With Scarborough at the zenith of its popularity as the most elegant seaside resort away from the south coast, the cricket during holiday time was always attended by huge crowds, swollen by local Yorkshiremen who came primarily to watch the giants of their county XI.

Yorkshire society and their guests congregated in the marquees put up for the festival along one side of the ground, and the scene here was described by Lord Londesborough's grandson, Osbert Sitwell, writing many years afterwards in his memoirs about one of his regular holiday visits to stay with his grandparents.

Chief of the treats (though never, alas, for me) was the Cricket Week, when

Scarborough: Wilfred Rhodes bowling for C.I. Thornton's XI against the
Australians during the 1902 festival.

Scarborough broke out into its greatest display, and there was feasting in the hot tents of the rich at the ground's edge. My grandfather, the founder and president delighted to entertain . . . The tents blazed with the ties of the cricketing clubs and the port-wine coloured faces of the *aficionados*, and between the rounds of cold salmon and cold chicken that were dispensed, we would have to sit solemnly and watch the progression – if such it can be called – of this, to me, always unattractive and lengthy game.

If he acquired a confirmed disinterest in the game, the young Osbert was greatly struck by the setting and atmosphere of the festival.

At Canterbury the cricket situation was slightly different, in that the matches were normal county games – usually the more important and prestigious fixtures – and the week came well before the end of the season. Although there may not have been quite the same holiday and festival air as at Scarborough, there was no denying the social importance in a county where cricket had deeper and more widely spread roots than in probably any other. In the early years of Canterbury week, in the mid-nineteenth century, some of the fixtures had involved I Zingari, whose members, along with those of the Band of Brothers, remained the most prominent among the crowds at Canterbury around the turn of the century, and the tradition of amateur plays in the evening, put on by the Old Stagers, a group affiliated to I Zingari, continued – as it does today.

Scarborough and Canterbury were annual social highlights in the two counties which reached a peak of elegance and popularity during the Edwardian period, but they were essentially provincial compared to the July fixtures at Lord's which were attended by London Society, and Eton v. Harrow was an event whose importance as part of the London Season was rivalled in the sporting world only by Royal Ascot. It became the kind of ritual that the Edwardians loved: dressing up in the maximum finery, carriages drawn up along the boundary, huge picnics and promenading around the ground at the luncheon interval, a picture of dazzling, if self-conscious, social display.

The most immediate difference between these matches and others at Lord's was the dramatically increased proportion of ladies among the spectators, and it was to a great extent their presence which made these such distinctive occasions, as E.V. Lucas described in a contemporary account of the University Match, published in 1898.

When Blue meets Blue the student of Lord's types is a little bewildered. His eyes are dazzled by the unfamiliar presence of fair ladies, who swarm around the ring, and, in the interval, all over the ground, like such a cloud of butterflies as one comes upon suddenly in a clear space in a wood on a hot August day. But none the less the types are there, hidden away maybe among summer fashions, pressed out from their accustomed places by this brightly hued, cheering, invading host. Where is the churl who would grumble at the presence of Beauty's Daughters at a cricket match? Let him come forward and be rebuked. True, they have hats that shut out yards of the pitch; true, their heads are so restless that it little avails him who sits behind to crane his neck either way; true, their use of the sunshade shows a lack of imaginative sympathy; true, they talk frivolously of the most serious deeds ever performed on the green spots of the earth . . .

Vignettes of Eton v. Harrow at Lord's in 1896.

As elegant and important as Ascot: Eton v. Harrow 1898.

There are three kinds of cricket-match girls: the girl who knows all about the game, who scores her brother's runs and keeps his bowling analysis, and takes not her eyes from the wickets while any play is to be seen; and the girl who is in a state of interested bewilderment; and the girl who watches the game with her back. The first is impatient of extraneous interferences; the second is not ungrateful for a little diversion; the third seeks it. 'Well played!' says (with no uncertain voice) the girl who knows. 'Is that man in the nightgown a don?' asks the second, pointing her parasol at the umpire. 'I prefer Sarah Bernhardt to Duse in *La Dame*,' says the third . . . A word more about Lord's ladies. Their hour of triumph is in the interval, and the proudest among them then are those who walk with a Blue.

In the same year that E.V. Lucas was describing the feminine invasion of the University Match the *Manchester Guardian* reported the Eton and Harrow match a few days later, showing the extent to which the match had become a Society event and sympathizing to some degree with those who deplored this development – and not missing the opportunity to have a characteristic swipe at the Lord's authorities.

Under the influence of the Eton v. Harrow match Lord's is transformed into something more than a cricket ground. It becomes the meeting-place of hundreds of old Etonians and Harrovians who have gathered from far and near to see the younger generation fight out their annual battle. Very pleasing it is to see portly respectabilities from the City, sunburnt colonels from the East, and rosy-cheeked squires shaking each

Less grand, more comfortable, but equally social:
Canterbury in 1901.

other warmly by the hand and recalling their school days in story after story. The fashionable world has taken the match under its expansive wing; Royalty has often honoured it by being present; and the ladies, as perhaps is only natural, have made it the occasion for a display of dress which almost rivals that in the Ascot enclosures on Cup-day. To keen cricketers this seems a degradation of a great match. As Lord Granby wrote last year in an indignant letter to the 'Times', cricket becomes subsidiary to 'carriages, corsets and chatter'. Indeed, the MCC would seem to deserve as severe a criticism for their arrangements in the Eton v. Harrow match as for the method in which they distribute the seats in the Oxford and Cambridge. The carriages are more numerous than ever, and do not give the general public the slightest opportunity of seeing even the top of an umpire's hat. It was generally understood that the big stand, which could not be opened in time to receive spectators in the inter-University match, would be ready to-day, but instead of being completed it has been entirely pulled down, though for what purpose it is impossible to imagine.

The great matches at Lord's and the festivals continued as healthy social occasions between the wars, but without quite the cachet which they were given in the Edwardian era by the atmosphere of unhurried leisure, the studied elegance and the elevation of cricket to a pinnacle where it could provide the setting for social activity. It was the disappearance of much of the leisure and the deflation of cricket's reputation to the levels of more mundane normality which largely accounted for the relative decline in country-house cricket after 1918. Whether in deckchairs around the boundary or anywhere else, country-house life as lived by the Edwardians did not survive the war and although country-house cricket continued to be played it was kept alive by devoted cricket enthusiasts and no longer part of a widespread way of life as it had been before 1914.

11

THE LUSTRE GENTLY FADES: 1910-14

The Edwardian era officially ended on 6 May 1910 when Edward VII died at Buckingham Palace in his 70th year. For the nine years of his reign, and for a decade or more before as Prince of Wales, he had presided over a period of incessant and lavish social activity: an opulent, regimented annual calendar of house-parties, garden-parties, balls, race-meetings and cricket matches. More than any other sports, racing and cricket were adopted by society, racing because it had always been the pastime of aristocrats and the rich; cricket because so many members of society played it or enjoyed it, mothers and dowager aunts took pride in the exploits of their sons and nephews and, whether on a carriage at Lord's or beneath an ancient cedar shading a country-house lawn, the game provided the setting for a social occasion.

Of course, this way of life did not come to an abrupt end with the death of its leading figure; it survived for another four years before being brought crashing down by the cataclysm of war. And while Royal Ascot in 1910 paid due respect to the recent departure of racing's most prestigious patron, with mourning dress compulsory in the royal enclosure, the scene a few weeks later at Lord's suggested that little if anything had changed. The traditional 'Lord's Week' of the University Match followed by Eton v. Harrow, after an interval of a couple of days when morning coats could be pressed and new dresses bought or chosen, saw sensation in both matches, the second of which has forever after been known as 'Fowler's Match', remembered with glowing pride by Old Etonians and glum despondency by Old Harrovians.

The University Match was equally dominated by one player, Philip Le Couteur, who, beyond his match-winning efforts at Lord's, was a figure of symbolic importance as one of the first Rhodes Scholars, a scheme which encapsulated much of the Edwardian ethos. In 1902 the mining entrepreneur, financier and imperialist Cecil Rhodes had died, leaving a fortune in excess of £6 million. The great majority of the money was given over to public service and his most lasting legacy was the Rhodes Scholarships to Oxford, open originally to students from the colonies who combined all-round academic and sporting talent. Le Couteur won his scholarship from Melbourne University and was a cricket blue for all three of his years at Oxford: 1909 to 1911.

In 1910 the start of the two-day match was delayed by heavy rain until the afternoon, but despite the conditions Le Couteur scored 160 in Oxford's first – and only – innings of 315. After they had been all out on the second morning, many spectators doubted that

Ally Sloper's view of Eton v. Harrow in 1897.

Agar's Plough at Eton (above) and the Upper Ground at Harrow (below), both photographed in 1895.

there was time enough for any result other than a draw, but after two hours Cambridge had been bowled out for 76, Le Couteur taking six for 20. In the follow-on they fared little better, struggling to 113, Le Couteur's leg-breaks again defeating them as he took five for 46. His 160 runs and match analysis of 11 for 66 enabled Oxford to win by the margin of an innings and 126 runs and was the best all-round performance the competition has ever seen.

If Le Couteur, as one of the first Rhodes Scholars, was a representative Edwardian figure, 'Fowler's Match' illustrated to an extraordinary degree the priorities of the Edwardian upper classes. Today it is hard to understand how a match between schoolboys, albeit a match that had, over a century or so, become something of an institution, could create so much excitement and at the time be regarded without any rival as the match of the season. But one has to look no further than H.S. Altham's *A History of Cricket* for confirmation of the game's legendary reputation. 'Inasmuch as there can never be a finer game of cricket than the Eton and Harrow match of 1910, I propose to cast proportion to the winds and describe it in some detail.' The strength of feeling aroused on both sides was demonstrated by Plum Warner's young wife who was among the crowd of thousands. At the nadir of Eton's fortunes, when they had slumped to 67 all out in reply to Harrow's commanding first innings score of 232, she turned to her neighbour and said with feeling, 'I shall not send my boy to Eton as they cannot play cricket,' and with that got up and left the ground in disgust. The drama which subsequently unfolded as she was travelling to her home in Kent was described by Cyril Foley, an Old Etonian, who had also left the ground at around the same time – equally unimpressed with what he had seen.

In Eton's second innings Robert St Leger Fowler, the captain, had restored some pride with an innings of 64 and from this point Foley gives a marvellous description of the remarkable change in fortune.

> The match was virtually over, Eton being only four runs ahead with one wicket to fall, and the 10,000 people who remained at Lord's did so solely for the convenience of eating their lunch there, and enjoying the sunshine ... After lunch the last Eton wicket, thanks to a great and plucky 40 not out by John Manners, added 50 runs, leaving Harrow exactly 55 to win.
>
> I was going to spend that Saturday to Monday at Coombe with General Sir Arthur Paget, and not being in the least anxious to see an overwhelming Harrow victory I left the ground and called in at White's Club to pick up my bag. Providentially, as it turned out, my hair wanted cutting. Halfway through the operation Lord Brackley looked in and said, 'Harrow have lost four wickets for 21 runs,' and a few minutes later: 'Harrow have lost six wickets for 21 runs.' That was enough. I sprang from the chair with my hair half cut and standing on end, and we rushed together into the street, jumping into a taxi and said: 'Lord's, double fare if you do it in 15 minutes.' We got there in 14 minutes 21 seconds (I carry a stopwatch), paid the man, and advanced on the pavilion at a pace which is called in the French Army '*le pas gymnastique*'.
>
> The shallow steps leading into the pavilion at Lord's form a right-angle. Round this angle I sprang three steps at a time, carrying my umbrella at the trail. A dejected Harrovian, wearing a dark-blue rosette, and evidently unable to bear the agony of the match any longer, was leaving the pavilion with bowed head. I was swinging my umbrella to give me impetus, and its point caught the unfortunate man in the lower part of his waistcoat, and rebounded from one of its buttons out of my hand and over the side rails of the pavilion. The impact was terrific, and the unlucky individual doubling up, sank like a wounded buffalo on to his knees, without, as far as I recollect, uttering a sound. I sprang over the body without apology, and shouting out instructions to George Bean, the Sussex pro., who was the gate attendant, to look after my umbrella, dashed into the pavilion and up the many steps to its very summit, where I hoped to find a vacant seat.

Lord's Ground.

ETON v. HARROW.

FRIDAY & SATURDAY, JULY 8, 9, 1910. (Two-Day Match.)

HARROW.	First Innings.		Second Innings.	
1 T. O. Jameson	c Lubbock, b Fowler	5	b Fowler	2
2 T. B. Wilson	b Kaye	53	b Fowler	0
3 G. W. V. Hopley	b Fowler	35	b Fowler	8
4 T. L. G. Turnbull	l b w, b Fowler	2	c Boswell, b Fowler	0
5 G. F. Earle .... (Capt.)	c Wigan, b Steel	20	c Wigan, b Fowler	13
6 W. T. Monckton	c Lubbock, b Stock	20	b Fowler	0
7 J. M. Hillyard	st Lubbock, b Fowler	62	c Kaye, b Fowler	0
8 C. H. B. Blount	c Holland, b Steel	4	c and b Steel	5
9 A. C. Straker	c Holland, b Steel	2	b Fowler	1
10 O. B. Graham	c and b Steel	6	not out	7
11 Hon. R. H. L. G. Alexander	not out	2	c Holland, b Steel	8
	B 18, l-b 2, w , n-b 1,	21	B 1, l-b , w , n-b ,	1
	Total	232	Total	45

FALL OF THE WICKETS.

1-15	2-84	3-88	4-121	5-133	6-166	7-191	8-201	9-216	10-232
1-0	2-8	3-8	4-21	5-21	6-21	7-26	8-29	9-32	10-45

ANALYSIS OF BOWLING.

Name.	1st Innings.						2nd Innings.					
	O.	M.	R.	W.	Wd.	N-b.	O.	M.	R.	W.	Wd.	N-b.
Fowler	37.3	9	90	4	...	...	10	2	23	8	...	...
Steel	31	11	69	4	...	...	6.4	1	12	2	...	...
Kaye	12	5	23	1	...	...	3	0	9	0	...	...
Stock	7	2	12	1	...	1	...	...	...	...	...	...
Boswell	8	4	17	0	...	...	...	...	...	...	...	...
	...	...	...	...	...	...	...	...	...	...	...	...

ETON.	First Innings.		Second Innings.	
1 R. H. Lubbock	l b w, b Earle	9	c Straker, b Hillyard	9
2 C. W. Tufnell	b Hillyard	5	l b w, b Alexander	7
3 W. T. Birchenough	c Hopley, b Graham	6	c Turnbull, b Jameson	22
4 W. T. Holland	c Hopley, b Hillyard	2	st Monckton, b Alexander	5
5 R. St. L. Fowler ...... (Capt.)	c Graham, b Jameson	21	c Earle, b Hillyard	64
6 A. I. Steel	b Graham	0	c Hopley, b Hillyard	6
7 D. G. Wigan	c Turnbull, b Jameson	8	b Graham	16
8 A. B. Stock	l b w, b Alexander	2	l b w, b Earle	0
9 Hon. J. N. Manners	c Graham b Alexander	4	not out	40
10 K. Lister Kaye	c Straker, b Alexander	0	c Jameson, b Earle	13
11 W. G. K. Boswell	not out	0	b Earle	32
	B 10, l-b , w 1, n-b	11	B 2, l-b , w 3, n-b	5
	Total	67	Total	219

FALL OF THE WICKETS.

1-16	2-16	3-26	4-34	5-36	6-57	7-62	8-64	9-66	10-67
1-12	2-19	3-41	4-47	5-65	6-107	7-164	8-166	9-169	10-219

ANALYSIS OF BOWLING.

Name.	1st Innings.						2nd Innings.					
	O.	M.	R.	W.	Wd.	N-b.	O.	M.	R.	W.	Wd.	N-b.
Earle	12	9	4	1	...	...	17.3	5	57	3	1	...
Hillyard	19	9	38	2	1	...	23	7	65	3	1	...
Graham	9	7	3	2	...	...	18	12	33	1	...	...
Jameson	4	1	4	2	...	...	9	1	26	1	...	...
Alexander	4.1	1	7	3	...	...	14	4	33	2	1	...
Wilson	...	...	...	...	...	...	2	2	0	0	...	...
	...	...	...	...	...	...						

Umpires—Moss and Whiteside.   Scorers—G. G. Hearne and Newman.

ETON WON BY 9 RUNS.

The scorecard for 'Fowler's Match', when schoolboy
cricket became the stuff of legend.

I arrived there at the moment that Jameson, the present Hampshire cricketer and ex-squash-racket champion, was lying on the ground badly cut over, and was told that he had been batting for forty minutes for no score. As he had always been such an exceptionally quick scorer, this is worthy of record. With the total at 29, Fowler yorked Straker for 1 (29–8–1). The excitement then reached its climax. I do not think I ever saw or heard anything like it. The roars from the Harrow stand whenever a run was made were heard in the Zoological Gardens [in Regent's Park]. Graham hit a 3, and then Fowler bowled Jameson. He had scored 2 and was ninth man out, and it was a thousand pities that he did not set up a record by carrying his bat through the innings for 0! (32–9–2). Alexander [later Field Marshal Earl Alexander of Tunis], who has recently taken over the Nowshera command in India, came in looking horribly confident. The score crept up slowly. By now the cheering had swollen into such a volume of sound that its overtones included Paddington Station as well as the Zoological Gardens in its perimeter. Thirteen priceless runs were sneaked or stolen by the indomitable last pair. How I loathed both of them! And just as things began to look really desperate, Alexander edged one to Holland in the slips off Steel and Eton had won by 9 runs!

In addition to his 64 Fowler had taken four wickets in the Eton first innings and then won the match by taking eight for 23 in the second.

The Oxford v. Cambridge game and 'Fowler's Match' demonstrated that amateur cricket as played at the universities and schools was as healthy and popular as ever, its considerable esteem as part of the national game unquestioned. But by the end of the new century's first decade the majority of the leading amateurs who gave the period its reputation had either given up first-class cricket – Stanley Jackson, Ranji, Lionel Palairet, Sammy Woods and C. J. Kortright, to name five of the best known – or were playing infrequently – Reggie Spooner, 'Tip' Foster and C.B. Fry – or, like Archie MacLaren, were not the players they had been five or ten years previously. In 1910 Lord Hawke relinquished the captaincy of Yorkshire after 28 seasons, and the following year Lord Harris played his last game for Kent, aged 60. In addition to the losses there seemed to be a dearth of young amateurs emerging with comparable dash and style, as well as the ability to take them into the top bracket increasingly dominated by professionals.

One player who stood out as an amateur in the best Edwardian traditions was F.R. Foster who, aged 22, in only his third season with Warwickshire and his first as their captain, led them to the most unexpected championship victory of the period, which in itself heralded a change in the first-class game. No county outside the leading six of Yorkshire, Lancashire, Nottinghamshire, Middlesex, Surrey and Kent had won the championship since 1871. Only a few places off the bottom in the previous three seasons, Warwickshire were unfashionable and, with the exception of Dick Lillee who retired during the 1911 season, had no player with a national reputation. As one newspaper commented after their victory, referring to two of the county's professionals, 'Ask the average follower of cricket what manner of man is Charlesworth or Baker and unless he comes from Warwickshire he will probably be at a loss.' Frank Foster's elevation to the captaincy of a side dominated by long-serving professionals – five of them were aged between 36 and 40 – was the master-stroke, as *Wisden* wrote at the end of the season, 'Not since W.G. Grace in the early days of the Gloucestershire Eleven has so young a captain been such a match-winning force.'

The only other amateurs with regular places in the side were twin brothers the same age as Foster, Frank and George Stephens, and it was Foster's ability to inspire his band of professionals – as well as his own play – which brought them victory. Foster himself

F.R. Foster (left), true to the best traditions of the Edwardian amateur, and
C.P. Mead (right), one of a new generation of professionals.

scored 1,614 runs at an average of 42 and took 141 wickets at an average of 20.31. The county could hardly believe their good fortune that they had managed to dissuade him against giving up first-class cricket which was his original intention at the end of the 1910 season and, as H.S. Altham wrote, as both player and personality he had all the qualities which had become hallmarks of the best amateurs.

If his bowling more than fulfilled all expectations, his batting far transcended them, and there was about all his cricket an atmosphere of supreme confidence and inexhaustible vitality that acted as a wonderful inspiration to his side. A brilliant batsman who attacked the bowling from the moment he went in, he played some astonishing innings, notably 300 in a single day against Worcestershire. In one less physically gifted such batting success might well have reacted on his bowling, but with Foster the one seemed to stimulate the other, and a century against Yorkshire but heralded the capture of 9 wickets in an innings.

Foster's achievements in 1911 won him a place in the England side to Australia in 1911–12, as did the batting of his senior pro, Septimus Paul Kinneir, who made his Test début at the age of 40, and the wicket-keeping of E.J. 'Tiger' Smith, aged 25. Smith had taken over from Dick Lillee for Warwickshire, and both men had learnt their cricket at the Cadbury works ground at Bournville. Kinneir only played in one Test of the tour but, in partnership with Sydney Barnes, Foster's left-arm fast-medium bowling won the series 4–1. Although Smith had originally been chosen as number two to Herbert Strudwick, he took over behind the stumps after the First Test on account of his association with Foster, whose left-arm-over bowling was notoriously difficult to keep wicket to. The decision paid off, not least in the Third Test when Smith stumped Clem Hill first ball off Foster in a move described by Warner as 'one of the technical masterpieces of the game'.

For the next three seasons victory in the county championship returned to normal,

Yorkshire, Kent and Surrey winning once each, but in 1912 almost as big a surprise as Warwickshire's victory the previous season came when Northamptonshire ran Yorkshire very close, to end up second. Admittedly the awful weather suited their bowling strength, but that alone would not have brought them ten wins and only one defeat in 18 matches. The decisive player was their professional all-rounder George Thompson, who had been with the county before they acquired first-class status. As H.S. Altham commented, 'This success, following immediately after Warwickshire's even more spectacular effort in the preceding year, was undoubtedly good for cricket in general and the competition in particular, for it made the public realize that the blue riband was not necessarily the monopoly of the famous and wealthy few.' All the same, Northamptonshire's play was definitely effective rather than exciting, as was already becoming more prevalent in county cricket and was to become increasingly the norm between the wars.

Other than the exhaustive but unsuccessful Triangular Tournament of 1912 there were no tours to England during the five seasons of 1910 to 1914, whereas from 1896 to 1909 inclusive there had been visitors each season. The lack of such distraction from the county championship only served to entrench its competitive nature. In such a climate it became increasingly difficult for amateurs to come in and out of county sides in the way they had previously done, and the inevitable result was that county cricket became inexorably more dominated by professionalism. In the past, the noticeable division between amateurs and professionals had been that the former could afford to take risks and play with panache, untroubled by the need to retain their place and thereby their living, whereas the latter were always guided to a greater or lesser extent by caution. Now, however, as the amateur contribution to the game began to decline – both in overall numbers and in the example of the leading players – so their style became less exalted as something for all cricketers to aspire towards. Safety became increasingly the watchword of batsmen, and Archie MacLaren was not the only member of the old guard to deplore the path he believed cricket was following. In an article which appeared in *The World of Cricket* he wrote: 'The majority of batsmen today absolutely decline to advance their left leg to the line of the well-pitched-up ball, for the purpose of driving it hard and true, as nine out of ten good players used to do.'

In 1913 the now portly and heavy-footed Tom Hayward overhauled one of W.G. Grace's most monumental milestones when he scored his 100th hundred. Nonetheless, W.G.'s total of 126 hundreds was still a long way off and Hayward, with only one more season to go, reached 104. He was still scoring his customary 1,000 every season but had some years previously handed over the mantle as England's foremost professional batsman to Jack Hobbs who had no rival as *the* individual player of the last few seasons before the war. Right up until 1914 Hobbs, the most accomplished batsman in England, demonstrated that safety need not be the watchword of successful batting and remained true to the traditions and style that had predominated when he was emerging as a player, using his lightning footwork and supple wrists to drive and cut the best that most bowlers could offer. The most simple compliment to the quality of his batting in this, the first phase of his career, came from Hobbs himself who, after his retirement, always hoped that he would be remembered for his batting prior to 1914 – even though it was between the wars that he went from one statistical milestone to the next.

In 1913 Hobbs enjoyed the most prolific season since he had joined Surrey, scoring 2,605 runs at an average of 50, and was only just pipped at the top of the season's averages by Phil Mead, the left-hander who had joined Hampshire the same year that Hobbs had arrived at The Oval, who was proving himself one of the most consistent of the new generation of professional batsmen. But in the midst of such professional reliability the 1913 season was given a welcome reminder of the gusto of Edwardian amateurism in a series of innings by the period's greatest entertainer, Gilbert Jessop. Jessop was now aged 39 but had already showed some of his old flair in games for Gloucestershire in 1913, before appearing for the Gentlemen against the Players at The Oval. In their first innings the Gentlemen collapsed to 28 for six when Jessop went in to bat, and ten runs later they had lost another wicket. Jessop obviously decided to repair the situation before he ran out of partners, and scored 81 in 70 minutes out of 111 runs added. When at one stage he on-drove J.W. Hearne over the main stand many old memories were stirred. In the second innings he enabled the Gentlemen to escape with a draw by scoring 107 in as many minutes.

Jessop had not originally been picked for the Gentlemen v. Players match two days later at Lord's, but his performance at The Oval almost demanded his inclusion, and in the event a vacancy came up when A.C. Johnstone was ill on the morning of the game. Nonetheless at such a late hour Jessop's appearance was by no means guaranteed — first he had to be found. Fortunately it was known that he would be going to Lord's as a spectator

The MCC side that toured Australia in 1911—12 and won convincingly 4—1.
Standing: (half shown) S.P. Kinneir, E.J. Smith, F.E. Woolley, S.F. Barnes,
J. Iremonger, C.P. Mead, J. Vine, H. Strudwick; seated: W. Rhodes,
J.W.H.T. Douglas, P.F. Warner, F.R. Foster, Gawley (manager), J.B. Hobbs,
G. Gunn; front: J.W. Hitch, J.W. Hearne.

and eventually he was spotted, informed of the developments, and whisked away to the dressing room. Jessop later described the comic situation in his memoirs.

> Though weaponless and without my own togs, it needed no pressure for me to enter once more into the enjoyments of another tilt with the 'Professors'. And so it came to pass when my turn arrived I waddled to the wicket closely embraced around the beam by an immaculate pair of 'Plum's' bags, feet concealed in a spare pair of Johnnie Douglas's boots – boats, I might almost say, for there was a keel on them almost the thickness of a mizzen-mast – and jauntily covering my sparse locks was a cap upon which were embroidered three scimitars.

Nervous about splitting the backside of Warner's flannels which were designed for a far slimmer frame than Jessop's, for once he was forced to abandon his habitual crouch at the wicket and adopt an uncomfortably upright stance. Jessop also explained that, 'the idea of undertaking that long trek back from the wicket to the pavilion in a ragged condition under the cool, critical eye of a London crowd forbade me taking any risk.' Despite the various hindrances Jessop made 63 off 58 balls in 70 minutes, which would have been rapid scoring for most of his contemporaries, until he holed out with a towering drive which Frank Woolley held on to. In the end the Players were bowled to victory by Sydney Barnes, who bowled Jessop for 1 and took seven for 38 in the second innings. Jessop's efforts had not gone unnoticed by the powers at Lord's and a few days after the match he received a courteous note from the MCC secretary.

> *Dear Jessop*
> *At a meeting of the committee held on Monday last I was instructed to write and offer you their thanks for so kindly accepting a place in the Gentlemen's side. They fully appreciate the sportsmanlike spirit you showed in helping them to make the side as representative as possible; probably at some personal inconvenience to yourself.*
>
> *Yours sincerely,*
> *F.E. Lacey*

There was one more Gentlemen v. Players fixture for Jessop to enliven, at the end-of-season Scarborough Festival in early September. As it turned out he used this match and the second of the festival, Lord Londesborough's XI against the champion county, Kent, to signal his departure from the game he had so enriched, with two vintage innings. In the first innings of the Gentlemen v. Players game, he scored 119 out of 172 runs made in just over 100 minutes, hitting 17 fours and 2 sixes and his side won a marvellously exciting match by six runs. Three days later he went in at number six for Lord Londesborough and savaged the very strong Kent bowling attack. In one over D.W. Carr was hit for 26 runs, including 3 sixes, and Jessop raced to his hundred in 55 minutes before being out on 116. Although Jessop played a few games for Gloucestershire in 1914 and for the Gentlemen at both The Oval and Lord's, these two innings at Scarborough were the last two first-class hundreds of his career. They provided a fitting conclusion to a career the like of which has never been seen since.

Kent's success in 1913, which saw them win the championship for the third time in five years, was only marred by one event early in the season brought about by an unwelcome intrusion of politics into the game. In April, in the sedate surroundings of Tunbridge Wells, a group of militant suffragettes set fire to the Nevill Ground's attractive pavilion – which was only a few years old – and razed it to the ground. It says much for the efficiency and determination of the Kent authorities that a replacement, built in identical style to the old one, was ready nine weeks later in time for the first match at Tunbridge Wells's cricket week, against Lancashire. Nor was this to be the suffragettes' only foray into England's sporting life: in June a far more serious disaster occurred when one of their supporters ran onto the course at Epsom during the Derby, in an attempt to bring down a runner owned by the king, and was so badly injured that she died three days later.

During the last few years before 1914 the unrest of the suffragette movement and other dissatisfied groups cracked the veneer of self-satisfied glamour which had spread thickly over Edwardian England. The enormous gap between the very rich and the very poor had been targeted by Lloyd George in his 'People's Budget' of 1909 and, other than the landed aristocracy who stood to lose by his proposals, most people agreed that the gap was too large. It would be naïve to suggest that cricket was directly affected by political and social issues, but as the pastime of tens of thousands – whether as players or spectators – it was closely influenced by the nation's mood and attitudes. As the sense of security and confidence which had fostered it and other institutions of Edwardianism retreated, so English cricket was bound to change.

At the same time the momentum of uninterrupted progress and expansion which had been a self-perpetuating force for nearly two decades was slowing down, and the personalities who had been responsible for so much of the game's gilded reputation became progressively fewer in number. Most of them had retired, but the premature deaths of a handful emphasized the losses. In 1912 Tom Richardson died in France aged 41; in 1913 the University Match was interrupted by two minutes' silence to mark the death a few days previously of Alfred Lyttelton, who had retired as a player before 1895 but who was throughout the period one of cricket's most illustrious figures; in May 1914 R.E. Foster died from diabetes aged 36, and two months later Albert Trott, the Australian who had once hoped to see snow at Lord's, shot himself in his lodgings in north London, aged 41. He had discharged himself from hospital suffering from terminal illness brought on by drinking. He was so impoverished when he died that the MCC had to pay for his funeral.

A number of the smaller counties sank into dire financial difficulties, and in May 1913 the MCC had to debate a proposal from Lancashire that a number of the weaker counties were dropped from the championship. Thanks largely to the influence of Lord Harris, who did not like the idea of the larger, richer counties bullying the others, the proposal was rejected. There were other areas of dissatisfaction. Most regularly and vociferously criticized was the style of play compared with that of a few years earlier: bowling and fielding designed to minimize stroke-play by batsmen, and batting which lacked vigour and any sense of adventure. From one quarter came a suggestion that all first-class games should be limited to two days in order to alleviate what was regarded as an unhealthily

Johnny Douglas (right) being seen off for the 1913—14 MCC tour to South Africa by Plum Warner and H.D.G. Leveson-Gower. His side achieved a crushing 4—0 victory in what proved to be the last pre-war tour.

crowded programme each summer. The idea was never adopted — although it was tried in 1919 — but such sentiments combined with the thinning ranks of amateurs to force out the various non-county fixtures, some of which had been afforded first-class status and many of which were played to first-class standards, which had so enriched the tapestry of Edwardian cricket and helped to maintain healthy contact between county cricket and the game at large.

Amateur cricket had one final flourish before the outbreak of war, when the Gentlemen beat the Players at Lord's by the decisive margin of 134 runs. They would not win again for twenty years, and the change in both their fortunes and the status of the fixture from the period 1895—1914 to the two decades between the wars is starkly illustrated by the comparative results for the games at Lord's. In the first period the Gentlemen had five wins, but between the wars could only manage two (the second when they were joined by Walter Hammond who had changed sides). Whereas only three games ended in a draw between 1895 and 1914, between the wars ten games were drawn.

The only sadness for the Gentlemen at Lord's in 1914 was that Reggie Spooner was forced by illness to drop out. He would never grace the competition again, other than in a single appearance at Scarborough in 1919, and it was fitting that he should have bowed out in the manner in which he had so often contributed to the matches, by scoring an inimitable 71 at The Oval a few days earlier. The game at Lord's was won by Johnny

A scene from the Lord's centenary match in 1914. King George V is talking to
Charles Fry, one of the captains. To their left is Lord Hawke and behind the
king are his two sons, the Prince of Wales and Prince Albert.

Douglas, as indeed it had largely been in 1911. Having revived the Gentlemen's batting in a partnership with S.G. Smith when they had collapsed to 73 for four in their first innings, Douglas proceeded to take nine for 105 in the Players' first innings, bowling without a rest for nearly four hours. After the Gentlemen had left the Players chasing 284 to win, Douglas and Frank Foster settled the matter, bowling them out for 150 and taking four wickets each.

Plum Warner reckoned that Douglas's medium-fast bowling was 'some of the finest seen in the history of these games' and exemplified both his formidable skill, which more than compensated for the occasional lack of excitement in his batting, and his fierce tenacity. Douglas was to continue his career after the war – although, at least as captain of England, he never enjoyed the successes of his pre-war years – but as Warner commented nostalgically at the end of his account of the game, 'In this last match before the First German War three great players made their farewell appearance in this series – C.B. Fry, G.L. Jessop and S.F. Barnes.'

A few weeks later, as war was declared on 4 August, Jack Hobbs was in the process of scoring 226 for Surrey against Nottinghamshire at The Oval, while at Lord's a 19-year-old called John Howell scored 78 for the Rest against Lord's Schools. Howell had just completed four years in the Repton XI which had shown him to be without question the most exciting schoolboy prospect in the country and a player with all the promise that had heralded the best amateurs of the past. Just over a year later he was killed in action in Flanders. As Howell's death signified the snuffing out of future promise, 1915 also witnessed the most symbolic evidence of the passing of an age with the deaths of W.G. Grace and Victor Trumper.

12

THE GOLDEN AGE: MYTH OR REALITY?

On the basis of records established and, in many cases still standing, the Edwardian period certainly qualifies as the Golden Age of cricket. Flicking through any analysis of statistical achievement, dates from the late 1890s and early 1900s crowd in: MacLaren's 424, Hirst's 2,000 runs–200 wickets double, Fry's six consecutive hundreds, Grace's 1,000 runs in May, Jessop's fast scoring, unbroken partnership records for most wickets, Blythe's 17 wickets in a day; all still at the top and many others very near. Of the 17 first-class counties, 12 made their highest innings totals during the period.

The plethora of high scores by both teams and individuals was partially accounted for by studiously prepared batting wickets and the declaration law (until 1910). The expansion of the annual programme of first-class cricket during the period provided considerably increased opportunities for record-breaking performances. And, putting a simplistic interpretation upon the various improvements in the game's organization that took place, one could argue that as cricket began to grow and expand at a previously unknown pace, so it naturally needed new bodies of control, new laws, new settings and clear parameters around the various levels at which it was played.

But neither statistics nor facts, however impressive they may be, are a satisfactory means of appraisal. They provide only a two-dimensional picture, and the vital element which they cannot portray is the spirit of an age, and herein lies the unique strength of the Edwardian years. For that spirit was one of intense vigour, born of a sense of discovery, of breaking new ground and appealing to new and vastly increased audiences, and encouraged by a society which lavished unstinting admiration upon sporting achievement. To excel as a cricketer was the ambition of thousands, while the gifted and privileged minority who emerged as the game's outstanding figures were motivated by healthy and questing ambition to explore and master both technique and performance of the game's various skills. Confident that theirs was a worthy and sought-after pastime, they lived up to high public expectation by consciously performing and providing entertainment and excitement.

There had been great players during the previous decades of the nineteenth century, but their cricket was technically primitive, lacking in versatility and stylistic variety and limited by poor pitches. With W.G. Grace showing the way almost single-handed for some years, their play provided the raw material that was, by the last years of the century, being developed and improved into the modern game to which, in the way it is played, there have been few beneficial additions since 1914. There were also great matches but, with the exception of the annual fixtures at Lord's, they took place in isolation from one another and were not part of a nationally organized institution.

Because cricket as a way of life and as part of the national way of life at many different levels was not questioned – rather the opposite: it was positively fêted – it enjoyed a state of fundamental good health which gave a firmer foundation than it has enjoyed at any other time. This basic healthiness meant that the disagreements, controversies and shortcomings – and there were plenty – although aired in heated debate and often causing bitterness and resentment, were never allowed to develop into a malaise that would eat away at the game's confidence and reputation.

The most regularly voiced criticisms of Edwardian cricket have been social: the gulf between Gentlemen and Players, shabby treatment of the professionals and the application of false social labels. But such criticisms have been levelled subsequently, whereas at the time, while there was plenty of room for argument over details, in principle cricket was seen to be organized by the standards of the day. Today it might seem positively tyrannical that Lord Harris chose new gardeners for Belmont, his country house in Kent, on their cricketing rather than their horticultural skill, and dragooned them into playing whenever he needed them, but to his contemporaries it would not have been at all unusual or offensive. By the same token Fred Root, one of the more outspoken professionals with scant respect for cricket's authorities or its social niceties, was quite happy as a young man to accept a job as the private coach to the son of Lady Warwick, whom he referred to as 'Lady Bountiful'. The relationship between cricket and social conditions is realistically assessed by Rowland Bowen who, arguing that cricket has fallen away ever since the Edwardian period, concluded that, 'if there are many others who disagree and who would have hated to have lived in that period, many of them, in turn, would have far rather played *and* watched cricket then than now.'

If the majority of professional cricketers had felt intense dissatisfaction with their way of life, their conditions and terms of work, and resentment at their enforced inferiority to amateur players, then they would never have scaled the heights in the manner that so many did. In addition to their ability, they demonstrated a capacity for hard work, many bowling hundreds, in some cases thousands of overs a season, which could not have been inspired by fear of unemployment alone. They were craftsmen, perfecting a combination of trade and art which, while it ensured their security and livelihood, also brought them prestige and accolade. The best were fully aware of their value and confident of their skill and, if few were as uncompromising about it as Sydney Barnes, all would have agreed with Wilfred Rhodes when, as coach at Harrow, he crossed swords with a self-opinionated master. Having accused the master of interfering, Rhodes went on, 'You can't know more about the game than me, you know', and when asked why not retorted, 'Because if you did you'd be playing for England and I'd be doing your job teaching Greek.'

Such robustness was widespread among Edwardian cricketers, professional and amateur alike; indeed it was a characteristic of the age when Englishmen in general considered they had much to be confident about. Germany might be threatening and the United States expanding to vast industrial and commercial power that would soon eclipse Great Britain's, but there was no questioning the international superiority of Britain and her empire and the fact that in most important matters Britain took the lead. Such a simplistic nationalist outlook was hardly surprising, given the background of decades of Victorian imperialism and the propaganda that people were fed by publications such as *Punch* and most of the cheap halfpennies, and in the music-halls.

Life in general was simple, so that major pastimes such as cricket loomed very large in the public awareness, as John Arlott explained, 'No graver matters weighed on the minds of any majority of the British public of the day to argue that a Test Match – or their village cricket match – was trivial.' It was also provincial and localized, without either modern communications or transport – of which the only effective national network was the railways. Test matches were attended by those who lived in or around the cities where they were held, or by the gentry who, by virtue of their comparative wealth, were able to enjoy far more mobility in their lives. For most cricket enthusiasts the county grounds were where they went to catch a glimpse of the heroes they so admired and, as Vic Marks has written, 'a cricket lover from Norton Fitzwarren would have been quite content to see Somerset lose to Sussex, provided Ranji scored a century'. Descriptions of matches and players filled column after column in the press, but photo-journalism was in its infancy and the majority of illustrations were line drawings or cartoons and most people did not read the newspapers anyway, they got to know the cricketers by collecting their pictures on cigarette cards.

Uninhibited by the commercialism which has increasingly dominated the modern era, national cricket was established specifically as a spectator sport. Paying attendances were the largest source of income for most county clubs, far outweighing the subscriptions of their members. Some counties, especially the less well-off, benefited from timely injections of funds from cricket-loving grandees, but it was only in times of emergency and would never have been considered a legitimate regular source of income. County stalwarts of the period would be appalled by the spectacle of a major fixture at Lord's or The Oval today, attended by at most a few hundred paying spectators and with the necessary income being generated by non-cricketing commerce in private boxes.

The players were conscious of their obligation to spectators that cricket should be enjoyable to watch as well as to play. If they forgot, on many grounds they would be swiftly reminded by caustic and vociferous barracking. The Yorkshiremen of Sheffield's grimy Bramall Lane were notorious, and as Jim Kilburn wrote in *Homes of Sport: Cricket*, 'to be condemned at Bramall Lane was a memorable and devastating experience'. Even in the supposedly more refined surroundings of Lord's, crowds were potentially volatile, as Archie MacLaren discovered to his cost in 1907 when he called off Lancashire's match with Middlesex, while across the river The Oval always had a reputation for more basic and earthy comment than the MCC's headquarters. In the last match of the 1912 Triangular Tournament, C.B. Fry upset a crowd of some 30,000 when, after heavy rain, he refused to accept an early start to the deciding match against Australia. When he went out to bat they booed almost to a man, and did so again when he appeared for the second innings. In the event he scored a match-saving 75 and the crowd enjoyed a complete change of heart and jostled in front of the pavilion cheering for Fry to appear. They were out of luck, and although the ever-diplomatic Ranji implored his friend to 'be his noble self' Fry would have none of it, 'It's not one of my noble days.'

Easily roused, crowds were equally easily pleased and, more important, appreciative and often discerning observers of the game. They enjoyed a battle of wits between Wilfred Rhodes and Johnny Tyldesley which went on for over after over as much as they enjoyed it when Tyldesley broke out and drove through the covers for four, or when Rhodes eventually broke through to take his wicket. The players themselves got used to playing in front of invariably large crowds which, for a county match of any importance, would always be a capacity attendance, and as a result strove to perform well, fast bowlers attacking and batsmen going for strokes. The atmosphere at county matches encouraged them to excel in every department of the game so that, at the end of the day, whoever won, the crowd had seen good and entertaining cricket.

A major test of the buoyancy and health of cricket was the manner in which bowlers responded to the quality of batsmanship with which they were confronted. Rather than being overawed and forced onto the defensive by the confident and attacking skill of batsmen, they replied in an equally positive manner by improving their various methods of delivery to the highest possible level. It was partially in response to the run-scoring capabilities of the batsmen and their desire to make scoring strokes against any kind of delivery that such a large quantity of the most impressive bowlers the game has seen appeared during the Edwardian period. Taking English bowlers alone, and only a selection of the best at that, no other period has produced such a combination of variety and quality as is represented by: Richardson, Lockwood, Kortright, Barnes, J.T. Hearne, F.R. Foster, Hirst, Rhodes, Haigh, Blythe and Bosanquet. The list does not include all-rounders usually better-known for their batting such as Jackson, Jessop and Crawford.

The quality of play in first-class cricket was high and the game was further enlivened by the individual personalities of many of the leading players so that, for instance in the case of a weak county such as Hampshire, their cricket was hugely popular thanks to the batting exploits of two of the amateur soldiers who invariably swelled their ranks, Captain E.G. Wynyard and Major R.M. Poore. Both were unforgettable figures: hugely tall, aggressive batsmen. Wynyard, who played for England in 1896, habitually wore an I Zingari cap secured by a strap under his chin, and he also bowled lobs. Poore enjoyed one astonishing season in 1899 when he scored over 1,500 runs at an average of 91. When he made his highest score of the season, 304, Wynyard made 225, and their stand of 411 remains the highest sixth-wicket partnership by Englishmen. For a number of years around the turn of the century they were a great attraction at Southampton, Portsmouth and Bournemouth and when they were able to join Hampshire on tour.

One major feature of Edwardian cricket, which was already disappearing by the last few years before 1914 and never reappeared again, was the manner in which first-class cricket retained links with the game at lower levels. Amateurs who made occasional appearances for counties played regular club and country-house cricket, while professionals often played in non-county matches at the end of the season. The effect of this strength of contact was described by Rowland Bowen, writing in *Cricket: A History* in 1970.

Thus there was an interchange of play between the great, the near-great and the not-so-great which is wholly absent nowadays, and which had not existed to such an extent since the final passing of the great All England Elevens and their progeny, in the early 1880s. First-class cricket was interwoven with minor county and club cricketers in this way and it went further: for the better clubs, touring or otherwise, invariably had some two-day fixtures in their programmes such as few are able to boast nowadays: inevitably a two-day game provided cricket of a better class.

In the final analysis it is perhaps this happy interrelation and the manner in which cricket was enjoyed and celebrated in such a range of surroundings which, as well as the glittering achievements of the great players, justify the Edwardian claim to be the Golden Age. It was the period of the most productive and far-reaching transition in the game's history, witnessing both the firm establishment of modern cricket as both game and organization, and pointing to where, in the future, its strengths and weaknesses would lie. At a crucial stage in the game's evolution it was adopted by a society whose way of life and priorities were ideally suited to foster it. The particular flavour and, for many people, the great charm of Edwardian cricket was provided by the amateurs, for never again would they be either secure or numerous enough to play with such dash and make such a significant contribution as they did then. They and the assured, leisured ease of the period were the most important elements subsequently to disappear, but they alone did not make it the Golden Age. It was the whole vibrant, progressive and totally assured picture of which they were part which justifies that description of the Edwardian period.

BIBLIOGRAPHY

Writing a book about a period of cricket which took place over 75 years ago means that first-hand personal reminiscences are rare. The great majority of my research has been from the books listed below, as well as from contemporary newspapers and periodicals. As well as the editions of *Wisden* there is a small number of books which, because they either deal specifically with the same period or are first-rate works on their particular subject, have proved invaluable and I would like to list them first.

Altham, H.S., *A History of Cricket* (London, 1926)
Bailey, Philip, *et al.*, *Who's Who of Cricketers* (London, 1984)
Bowen, Rowland, *Cricket: A History* (London, 1970)
Morrah, Patrick, *The Golden Age of Cricket* (London, 1967)
Pollard, Jack, *The Turbulent Years of Australian Cricket, 1893–1917* (London, 1987)
Sissons, Ric, *The Players* (London, 1988)
Wisden Book of Obituaries (London, 1986)
Wisden Book of Cricket Records (London, 1986)

Birley, Derek, *The Willow Wand* (London, 1979)
Bright-Holmes, John (ed.), *The Joy of Cricket* (London, 1984)
Bright-Holmes, John (ed.), *Lords and Commons* (London, 1988)
Brodribb, Gerald, *The Croucher* (London, 1974)
Brodribb, Gerald, *Next Man In* (London, 1985)
Brodribb, Gerald, *Cricket at Hastings* (London, 1989)
Brown, L.H., *Victor Trumper and the 1902 Australians* (London, 1981)
Cardus, Neville, *Days In the Sun* (London, 1924)
Cardus, Neville, *Cricket* (London, 1930)
Cardus, Neville, *English Cricket* (London, 1945)
Cardus, Neville, *Cricket All the Year* (London, 1952)
Chesterton, G. and H. Doggart, *Oxford and Cambridge Cricket* (London, 1989)
Coldham, J.D., *Lord Harris* (London, 1983)
Cornwallis-West, G., *Edwardian Hey-Days* (London, 1930)
Darwin, Bernard, *W.G. Grace* (London, 1934)
Down, Michael, *Archie. A Biography of A.C. MacLaren* (London, 1981)
Engel, Matthew (ed.), *The Guardian Book of Cricket* (London, 1986)
Foley, C.P., *Autumn Foliage* (London, 1935)
Frindall, Bill, *Wisden Book of Test Cricket* (London, 1978)
Frindall, Bill, *England Test Cricketers* (London, 1989)
Frith, David, *The Golden Age of Cricket, 1890–1914* (London, 1978)
Fry, C.B., *Life Worth Living* (London, 1939)
Gibson, Alan, *Jackson's Year* (London, 1965)

Gordon, Sir Home (Bt), *Background of Cricket* (London, 1939)

Grace, W.G., *Cricketing Reminiscences* (London, 1899)

Green, Benny, *A History of Cricket* (London, 1988)

Hart-Davis, Rupert (ed.), *The Essential Neville Cardus* (London, 1949)

Hobbs, J.B., *My Cricket Memories* (London, 1924)

Hodgson, R.L., *Cricket Memories* (London, 1930)

Jessop, G.L., *A Cricketer's Log* (London, 1922)

Kay, John, *Cricket in the Leagues* (London, 1970)

Lewis, Tony, *Double Century* (London, 1987)

Lucas, E.V., *Cricket All His Life* (London, 1950)

Lyttelton, George and Rupert Hart-Davis, *Letters* (London, 1897)

Macartney, C.G., *My Cricketing Days* (London, 1930)

Marks, Vic, *Wisden Illustrated History of Cricket* (London, 1989)

Midwinter, Eric, *W.G. Grace. His Life and Times* (London, 1981)

Nicole, C.R., *West Indian Cricket* (London, 1957)

Nowell-Smith, S. (ed.), *Edwardian England 1901–10* (London, 1964)

Padwick, E.W., *A Bibliography of Cricket* (London, 1984)

Ranjitsinhji, K.S., *The Jubilee Book of Cricket* (London, 1898)

Rogerson, Sidney, *Wilfred Rhodes, Professional and Gentleman* (London, 1960)

Root, Fred, *A Cricket Pro's Lot* (London, 1937)

Ross, Alan, *Ranji, Prince of Cricketers* (London, 1983)

Sitwell, Osbert, *Left Hand Right Hand!* (London, 1945)

Swanton, E.W. (ed.), *Barclays World of Cricket* (London, 1986)

Swanton, E.W., *Back Page Cricket* (London, 1987)

Trevor, Colonel Philip, *Cricket and Cricketers* (London, 1921)

Warner, Sir Pelham, *Gentlemen and Players 1806–1949* (London, 1950)

Warner, Sir Pelham, *Long Innings* (London, 1951)

Webber, Roy, *The County Cricket Championship* (London, 1957)

Webber, Roy, *The Phoenix History of Cricket* (London, 1960)

Williams, Marcus (ed.), *The Way to Lord's* (London, 1983)

Woods, S.M.J., *My Reminiscences* (London, 1925)

Wynne-Thomas, Peter, *Give Me Arthur* (London, 1985)

INDEX

Numerals in *italics* refer to illustrations